英汉对照

A New Translation and Interpretation of *The Analects*
《论语》今译新解

党争胜　毛艳君　译著
Lucian X. Lu 审校

西北工业大学出版社

【内容简介】《〈论语〉今译新解》以《论语》全本为蓝本,择取其中关于"为学"、'修身"、"仁道"、"礼乐"、"财富"、"孝悌"、"交友"、"处世"、"为政""教育"和"生死"等十三个方面的话题内容编辑成书。为帮助读者理解,同时也为了将《论语》的思想和智慧推广到世界,我们在编辑的过程中结合国内名家的研究对原文进行了语内和语际翻译,并对每一条语录进行了启发性的延展解读。对这些解读,我们也附上了英语翻译,希望能对有志于学习和研究中国文化的外国读者有益。

图书在版编目(CIP)数据

《论语》今译新解:英语/党争胜,毛艳君译著.
—西安:西北工业大学出版社,2016.3
ISBN 978-7-5612-4785-3

Ⅰ.①论… Ⅱ.①党… ②毛… Ⅲ.①儒家 ②《论语》—译文—英文 ③《论语》—注释—英文 Ⅳ.①B222.2

中国版本图书馆CIP数据核字(2016)第057246号

出版发行:	西北工业大学出版社
通信地址:	西安市友谊西路127号 邮编:710072
电 话:	(029) 88493844 88491757
网 址:	www.nwpup.com
印 刷 者:	陕西天意印务有限责任公司
开 本:	889 mm×1 194 mm 1/32
印 张:	7
字 数:	149千字
版 次:	2016年3月第1版 2016年3月第1次印刷
定 价:	25.00元

序 言
Preface

  《论语》是记述孔子及其弟子言行的一部书，体现的是儒家创始人孔子的重要思想。在中国文化史上，孔子有着千古不灭的光辉一页：他首开学堂，广纳门徒，成为第一个伟大的教育家；编修了《诗》、《书》、《礼》、《乐》、《易》、《春秋》等六部典籍，传承了古代文明。由他创立的儒家学派，在中国几千年的文化史中独树一帜，为整个中国封建社会的主流思想奠定根基。可以毫不夸张地说，儒家思想构成了中国传统文化调色板的主要色彩，是中华民族共同的人生哲学。

  作为中国古代思想文化的重要结晶，《论语》对中华民族几千年的历史文化产生了浃肌透骨的深刻影响，它本身也成为中国传统文化的一个重要而珍贵的组成部分。《论语》确立以人为核心的道德思想体系，提出孝、悌、忠、信、恭、宽、敏、勇、直等一系列完整道德规范。在《论语》中，有关修身养性、仁义孝悌的道德学说最为殊胜，反映了孔子以德处事、为仁由己、身体力行的道德自觉理想。今天，我们尽可站在不同角度去解释它、研究它、扬弃它，给它以种种批判或肯定，但我们绝不可轻视它、否定它甚至像历史上某些时期那样曲解它。从继承传统文化、吸收儒家思想的合理成分这一出发点来看，我们必须始终给它以足够的珍视，因为它不仅曾经在中国的历史文化长河中熠熠生光、惠及时人，其中许多重要思想在今天看来也仍然具有"恢复文化自信，构建民族精神支柱，传承国学命脉，提升国民素质和国家'软实力'"的时代价值。

就个人而言，阅读像《论语》这样的国学经典也是阅读其他读物不可替代的。国学经典，譬如《诗经》、《论语》、《孟子》、《道德经》、《资治通鉴》、《孙子兵法》、《山海经》等等，是千百年传承下来的中国传统学术文化的不朽之作，既可经世致用，也可修身养性，从中学会做人处世的道理、树立齐家治国的崇高理想，这对人生成长和事业的成功无疑至关重要。因此，阅读经典，应当是一个人人生修养追求的一种境界，一个追求道德升华的"君子"的教育目标。重读《论语》，我们应当继承、吸取其精华，并赋予它新的时代内容，以提高全民族甚至是全人类的道德意识、责任感和使命感，这才是学习、研究《论语》的现代价值所在，也是我们注释、翻译它的初衷所在。

在翻译和注释《论语》的过程中，我们参考和借鉴了几部已出版的英译《论语》中的部分译法，在此对前辈的译绩致以深深的敬意。Lucian X. Lu（吕新安）教授对全书进行了审校，

序 言

张生庭教授等参加了校对核红等工作,我们在此表示谢意!西北工业大学出版社李东红编辑在本书的出版过程中付出了大量心血,在此一并表示感谢!

由于认识和能力所限,我们对《论语》的阐释和翻译还不够精确,书中可能存在一些不足和甚至讹误,恳切盼望有识之士不吝批评,惠赐雅正,以便及时修订。对读者诸君的批评,我们在此先致谢意。

党争胜

2015年9月于西安外国语大学

目 录
Contents

一、为学（To Learn） …………………………………… 1
二、修身（Self-Edification）…………………………… 28
三、仁道（The Way to Virtue）………………………… 56
四、礼乐（Ritual and Music）………………………… 73
五、理想（Ideals）……………………………………… 85
六、财富（Wealth）……………………………………… 96
七、孝悌（Filial Piety and Fraternal Submission）…… 107
八、交友（Making Friends）…………………………… 125
九、处世（Conducting Oneself in Society）…………… 132
十、为政（Administration）…………………………… 164
十一、教育（Education）……………………………… 182
十二、生死（Life and Death）………………………… 196
十三、孔子其人（Confucius —— the Man）………… 202

一、为 学（To Learn）

1. 子曰："学而时习之，不亦说乎？有朋自远方来，不亦乐乎？人不知，而不愠，不亦君子乎？"

今 译

孔子说："学了并能经常实践，不也很快乐吗？有共同见解的人从远方来，不也很快乐吗？不为他人所理解而不怨恨，不也是君子的风范吗？"

Translation:

The Master says, "Isn't it a pleasure to learn and put what you have learnt to practice? Isn't it a delight to receive a friend sharing common viewpoints coming from afar? Isn't he a gentleman who does not grudge against those who do not understand him?"

新 解

  学习是人天生的能力，人通过学习唤醒潜能，并在这过程中享受快乐。在学习方法上，孔子认为"学"要和"习"结合起来，学以致用，当我们将所学到的知识应用到实践中，并且取得一定的效果，我们就会享受到一种有所收获的快乐，就不会把学习当成一种苦差事。朋友就是另外一个自己，可以在他面前尽情地吐露心思，与朋友在一起还可以相互印证、相互启发，那种惊喜、愉悦的心情我们每个人都有所体会。我们不能要求所有人都站在我们的角度考虑问题，当不被别人理解的时候，我们应该用宽广的胸怀去接受。真正的君子，应该有开阔的心胸，即使别人不理解，也不要气急败坏，泰然处之不是尽显君子风度吗？ 这一章作为《论语》的首章，揭示了作为一个人一生所应追求的快乐。

Contemporary interpretation:

  Being able to learn is humankind's inborn ability. Learning wakens the dormant aptitude and offers the learner joy. So far as learning approaches are concerned, Confucius thought that learning, to be effective, should be coupled with practice. If we put what we have learnt to practice and find the result beneficial, we will experience the harvesting pleasure from the process and will not regard the learning process an ordeal any more. Our friends may serve as our own reflections. To them we could bare our heart and soul. With them we could examine our thoughts and aspirations. In the process of communication each of us could experience the surprising delight. And we should not expect all of the people think the same way as we do. When we are misunderstood, we should accept it with an open mind. A gentleman should be receptive-minded. Even being misunderstood, he should not fly into a rage. Calmness and composure mirror a gentleman's true self. This chapter, as the first of *The Analects*, tells us what kind of pleasure a person should pursue all through his life.

2. 子夏曰:"贤贤易色;事父母,能竭其力,事君,能致其身;与朋友交,言而有信。虽曰未学,吾必谓之学矣。"

今 译

子夏说:"敬重德行而不看重容貌,侍奉父母能竭尽其力,侍奉君主能奉献出自己的生命,与朋友交往言而有信。即使自称未曾学习,我必定说他学了。"

Translation:

Zixia says, "Prizing the virtue over the looks, devoting one's all to parents, sparing not even one's life for the monarch, and true with every word to one's friends makes a man learned despite his self-claimed modesty in learning."

新 解

　　子夏认为，对贤德之人恭敬，对父母尽孝，对君主尽忠，对朋友守信，这样的人即使没有读书，也可以被认为是有学问了。这里同样强调的是做人的重要性。学习知识不是目的，应用才是目的。知识的学习要实践，要身体力行，如果达到了这种要求，就等于是学了。

Contemporary interpretation:

　　The statement above actually emphasizes the importance of playing a true man. According to Zixia, acquiring knowledge should not be a person's final aim. Rather, applying the knowledge to practice should be. A person must put what he has learnt into practice. Such practice, even without possession of knowledge, is equivalent to knowledge.

---

3. 子曰："君子食无求饱，居无求安，敏于事而慎于言，就有道而正焉，可谓好学也已。"

今 译

　　孔子说："君子饮食不要求饱，居住不要求舒适，敏捷处事而谨慎言语，请求有道者匡正，可以说是好学了。"

一、为 学（To Learn）

Translation:

The Master says, "A gentleman is temperate in eating, austere in living, prompt in act, and prudent in speech. He rectifies himself by learning from the virtuous persons. Such a person could be said to have a taste for learning."

新　解

这是君子修养的一个标准。要成为君子，首先不应追求物质生活的享受，而应该把注意力放在塑造自己的道德品质方面，追求精神境界的升华。跟外界接触时也应遵守准则，做事勤勉，说话谨慎。另外，"近朱者赤，近墨者黑"，"物以类聚，人以群分"，结交人也要有所选择，尽量接近有"德行"的人，这样才能看到自己的不足，提升自己，这也是自我学习的一个重要方面。

Contemporary interpretation:

This statement offers a benchmark to measure a gentleman. To be a gentleman, a person needs to be insouciant with materialistic pursuits, but earnest with the cultivation of a virtuous character. When he communicates with the others, he should abide by the principle of "doing more and speaking less". When making friends, he should remember the sayings of "He that lives with cripples learns to limp" and "Birds of a feather flock together", trying his best to approach those virtuous people. Only in this way can he find his shortcomings and perfect himself. This, as a matter of fact, is an important aspect of self-teaching.

4. 子曰："君子不器。"

今译

孔子说："君子不能像器具那样，只有某一方面的用途。"

Translation:

The Master says, "Unlike a utensil, the gentleman is not designed for but one use."

新解

孔子在这里强调人们在自我培养、自我修身时不能只注重单一的一种能力，更应该全面发展自己的个性、才能，掌握多方面的知识，使自我价值在不同领域实现。

Contemporary interpretation:

Here Confucius admonishes that a gentleman is made for more than one specific purpose. He should master knowledge about various disciplines and develop his characters and abilities in many ways so as to fulfill his values in different fields.

一、为 学（To Learn）

> 5. 子曰："学而不思则罔，思而不学则殆。"

今 译

孔子说："学习而不思考，则将毫无领悟；思考而不学习，就会陷于迷惑。"

Translation:

The Master says, "To study without thinking will breed vacuity; to think without learning will breed bewilderment."

新 解

孔子主张学思结合。学而不思就成了不能融会贯通的"书呆子"，同样，思而不学就容易陷入以往的经验和主观判断。当今时代不停发展，人事日新月异，过去的经验可能会变成今天的绊脚石。只有将学与思结合，才能令自己具备发展的眼光和思维。

Contemporary interpretation:

Confucius advocates marriage between learning and thinking. If one just learns and does not think actively, he will become a pedant. Similarly, if he just thinks and does not learn, he will elapse into a dependence on outmoded experience and become too subjective. Times fly and things change. Yesterday's experience may become today's tumbling stone. Only by combining learning with thinking can a person develop a dynamic vision for the future.

6. 子曰："由，诲汝知之乎？知之为知之，不知为不知，是知也！"

今 译

孔子说："由啊，我所教的你明白了吗？知道的是知道的，不知道的是不知道的，这就是智慧啊。"

Translation:

The Master says: "Zilu, this do you know? If you know it, confess so; if you do not know it, confess so. Then you really know."

新 解

人的知识再丰富，学识再渊博，也总有不懂的问题。所以人必须有实事求是的态度，学而知，问而知，才能学到更多的知识，才能更加完善自己。如果不懂装懂，强不知以为知，自欺欺人，那是非常愚蠢的。

一、为 学（To Learn）

Contemporary interpretation:

A person, no matter how much he knows, will find much more that he does not know. Accordingly, every one of us should take a matter-of-fact attitude toward learning. Only by consistent learning and probing can we have a good command of knowledge and have ourselves improved. It is self-deceiving and very foolish to pretend to know what we really do not know.

> 7. 子曰："知之者，不如好之者。好之者，不如乐之者。"

今 译

孔子说："对于学问事业，了解它的人不如爱好它的人，爱好它的人不如以它为乐的人。"

Translation:

The Master says, "To know is not so good as to love to know. To love to know is not so good as to rejoice to know."

新 解

本章中提出学习明道的三种由浅入深的不同境界：知之、

好之、乐之。确实如此,人们在学习、工作、事业等各个方面,只要是有所追求的话,对它了解的人总是比不上爱好它的人,爱好它的人又总是比不上以此为乐的人。最让我们欣然接受的当然是能够使我们得到享乐的东西了。

Contemporary interpretation:

Here Confucius suggests a three-step process of learning, each representing a higher level than the previous one, namely, to know about something, to have an interest in it and to delight in it. Undeniably, a person's utmost delight comes from the things in which he can find joy.

---

8. 子曰:"三人行,必有我师焉:择其善者而从之,其不善者而改之。"

今 译

孔子说:"几个人在一起走路,一定有我的老师在那里。选择他们好的地方向他们学习,不好的地方,就改正它。"

Translation:

The Master says, "In the company of any three people, there must be a teacher for me. I shall learn what is good about them and admonish myself against what is not good about them."

新 解

这是孔子的一句名言,流传至今,仍有其强大的生命力。真正懂得学习的人便是这样:一方面学无常师,每个人身上都有优缺点,这样利用一切机会自觉丰富自己,随处向别人学习,取其所长,以提高自己的道德修养;另一方面学习不光是在死的书本上下功夫,还要在社会上观察:别人对的地方要学习,不对的地方也是自我检查改正的老师,要以别人的错误为借鉴,吸取教训,以免重蹈覆辙。

Contemporary interpretation:

This famous aphorism by Confucius, though bequeathed to us from distant history, still has its vitality of reason. This aphorism delineates the real learner: If a person wants to increase his knowledge and lift his morality, he should avail himself of every chance to learn from those who are in his company and are better than him in a certain aspect. The aphorism also exhorts that knowledge should not passively come from books alone, but from social observation, from an emulation of others' merits, and from an admonition against others' demerits, for the purpose of not repeating the same mistake.

9. 曾子曰:"士不可以不弘毅,任重而道远。仁以为己任,不亦重乎?死而后已,不亦远乎?"

今 译

曾子说:"读书人不可以不胸怀宽广而意志刚强。他们任务重大而道路遥远。把实行仁德作为自己的责任,这个责任不也是很沉重吗?奋斗到死才停止,这个历程不也是很遥远吗?"

Translation:

Master Zeng says, "A man of letters must possess magnanimity and tenacity as their onus is onerous and their journey long. Isn't the obligation grave when the pursuit is after virtue and benevolence? Isn't the journey long when the struggle ceases not till last breath?"

新 解

曾子提出"弘、毅"作为士求仁的要求。"弘"就是要有宽广的胸襟,宏大的气度,目光远大而包容一切。"毅",就是要有坚强的意志,不拔的毅力,果敢的决断,目光犀利而处事利落。读书人想要担当起实行仁德的重任,为国家社会做出贡献,就必须身体力行,持之以恒,死而后已,才可以达到仁的境界而成为君子。这段话正是古代读书人的使命意识和道义意识的精彩表达,千百年来一直成为鼓舞士大夫们自强不息、以天下为己任的经典格言。

一、为 学 (To Learn)

Contemporary interpretation:

Master Zeng puts forth magnanimity and tenacity as requirements for the man of letters. Magnanimity means a generous spirit and vision that is inclusive of all. Tenacity means buoyancy, decisiveness, and an incisive promptitude. If a man of knowledge wants to devote himself to the country and shoulder the responsibility of practicing benevolence, he must persistently carry out his duty and never swerve before he dies. This is the sole way to sublimate one into a gentleman. The adage is a brilliant delineation of the ancient cultured man with a keen awareness of moral responsibility. For eons, this classical aphorism has been inspiring upright scholars and civil servants to tenaciously fulfill their moral responsibility for the society.

---

10. 子曰:"学如不及,犹恐失之。"

今 译

孔子说:"追求学问好像永远赶不上,学到了一点知识还担心失去。"

Translation:

The Master says, "I fear not to keep the pace in learning; I fear more to forget the little I have learned."

新解

学如逆水行舟,不进则退,道德、学问的追求是没有止境的。"学如不及"是说要掌握知识,应该随时感到不充实,不满足,知道"学海无涯","不进则退",要奋发追求,持之以恒。如果没有这样的心情,懂得一点就心满意足,结果就是退步。"犹恐失之"是如何巩固知识的问题。学到知识后要经常复习、实践,才能牢固地掌握它。孔子的这句话,勉励人们学习一点儿都不能松懈,要时刻警觉自己,不断下苦功夫追求,才能学有所成。

Contemporary interpretation:

Learning is like rowing a boat upstream against the current; if you do not progress, you regress. The pursuit of knowledge and virtue should never end. By "I worry that I cannot learn fast enough" Confucius means that, in pursuit of knowledge, we should practice a voracious appetite and a reluctant satisfaction. We should know that the sea of knowledge is boundless. Therefore, we must work hard and accumulate knowledge persistently. A smattering of knowledge and easy satisfaction are equivalent to regression. By "I also worry that I may forget what I have learned" Confucius actually addresses the issue of consolidating the acquired knowledge. Only by repeatedly reviewing and practicing the already-acquired knowledge can we have a good command of it. The exhortation here is that accomplishment in learning requires constant awareness and studious pursuits.

一、为 学 (To Learn)

11. 子曰："譬如为山，未成一篑，止，吾止也。譬如平地，虽覆一篑，进，吾往也。"

今 译

孔子说："比如堆一座山，只要再加一筐土就能成功，但停止了，这是我自己停止的。比如用土平地，虽然只倒下一筐土，但立志前进，这是我自己要前进的。"

Translation:

The Master says, "Like raising a mound, if I stopped short of the last needed basketful of dirt, the failure of incompletion is mine; like filling a pit, even though there is only one single basketful of dirt dumped, the will of success is mine as well."

新 解

孔子借《书经》这"为山九仞，功亏一篑"的话为喻，告诫学生为学、求道贵在坚持，持之以恒，则积少成多；中道而止，则前功尽弃。《老子》也有类似的话说："民之从事，常于几成而败之。故慎终如始，则无败事矣。"意思是成功在望时，人们常常因放松对自己的要求而功亏一篑。"行百里而半九十"，学问、事业都是一步步积累而成的，不能半途而废。只有持之

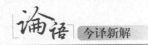

以恒，才能有所成就。一切的作为、成功或失败，都在于自己，不要推卸到外来的因素。

Contemporary interpretation:

Borrowing this aphorism from Analects, Confucius admonishes his students not to give up half-way in their process of pursuit of knowledge and truth. Success comes from a person's stamina and perseverance, and it fails with his giving-up half-way. Laozi actually has said almost the same words: "Some people usually stop at where they are near the success. If we could do things the same way as we have started it, we will meet no failure." That is to say, a one-hundred-mile journey might be left unfinished just because the traveler gives up after he has travelled ninety miles. So we must remember that whatever we engage in, the outcome lies with us. We cannot blame others for our own failure.

---

12. 子夏为莒父宰，问政。子曰："无欲速，无见小利。欲速则不达，见小利则大事不成。"

今 译

子夏担任莒父的县长，请教政治的做法。孔子说："不要想要很快收效，也不要只看小的利益。想要很快收效，反而达

一、为　学（To Learn）

不到目的，只看小的利益，反而办不成大事。"

Translation:

When Zixia, the Governor of Jufu County, counsels Confucius on statecraft, the Master says, "Seek neither the speed nor the petty profit. The former thwarts the final goal; the latter, the great cause."

新　解

这章中孔子教育子夏，为政要目光远大，不能急于求成，不要贪图小利。确实这样，施政要循序渐进，事情想要有圆满的结果，需要内部、外部的条件配合。条件不具备，心急也没有用，如果求速成往往反而达不到目的。不要在一些小利益上花费太多心力，要顾全到整体大局，贪图小利反而会因小失大。

Contemporary interpretation:

In this chapter, Confucius teaches Zixia the importance of vision, patience, and magnanimity to effective statecraft. If he wants to accomplish something, he must make progress in planned steps. Hasty actions and rush decisions could only lead to a contrary end. Success with a great cause requires sight of the big picture; excessive attention to trifles gains the penny and loses the pound.

13. 子曰："古之学者为己，今之学者为人。"

今 译

孔子说:"古代学者注意个人道德品质修养,不图虚名,今之学者为了炫耀自己,务求虚名。"

Translation:

The Master says, "The ancient scholars emphasized moral lift and so they learn, seeking no fame; in contrast, the contemporary scholars value big-name list and so they learn, seeking but fame."

新 解

孔子在本章中提出了为学的两种态度,一是为己,就是为了提高自己的道德品质修养,身体力行,学以致用。一是为人,就是不求实学,只为装饰门面,炫耀于人。我们现在的很多人上学,自己没有一点兴趣,只是为了家人的荣耀而读书,或者是为了混一张文凭,或者把读书作为一种可以炫耀的谈资。如果是抱着这样的目的求学,那么怎么可能踏踏实实地读书呢?当然,不管怎么样,只要愿意读书都不是坏事。

Contemporary interpretation:

In the statement, Confucius puts forward two attitudes toward learning. One type of people uses learning to achieve edification of the character and amelioration of the action. The other type of people learns to embellish their name and to parade their knowledge. Nowadays, many go to school not because of an interest in learning, but for glory to their family name or for the diploma or for pretense.

一、为 学 (To Learn)

Such an attitude defeats honest and effective learning. An interest in learning, after all, is not a bad thing.

---

14. 子贡问为仁。子曰:"工欲善其事,必先利其器。居是邦也,事其大夫之贤者,友其士之仁者。"

今 译

子贡问如何培养仁德。孔子说:"工匠要想做好他的工作,首先一定要把工具磨锋利。住在哪个国家里,应该侍奉那个国家大夫中有贤德的人,与那个国家中有仁德的士人交朋友。"

Translation:

Zigong asks about virtue, and the Master says, "Sharpen your tool to quicken your work. Residing in their state, you should serve the virtuous ones of nobility and befriend the virtuous ones of obscurity."

新 解

本章中孔子用工匠使用工具以成事为喻,因势利导教导子贡求仁之道,教育他一个人要修养仁德,一定要结交贤者,得到师友的切磋琢磨之助,切勿自以为是,自视甚高。在现代社会也是这样,交朋友要结交那些能够给予自己启发帮助的贤才。

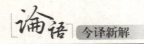

读书也是同理,要多读书、读好书,能够从书中学到知识,得到真知灼见。

Contemporary interpretation:

In this statement Confucius uses the analogy of the craftsman's tool to teach Zigong to make friends with those who are virtuous and learned. And he admonishes Zigong not to appear to be supercilious and arrogant. Such wisdom of Confucius applies to the modern society as well. We should make good friends and read good books, for good friends inspire in us wisdom and good books instill in us knowledge.

15. 子曰:"吾尝终日不食,终夜不寝,以思,无益,不如学也。"

今 译

孔子说:"我曾经整天不吃东西,整夜不睡觉,用来思考问题,但没有收益,还不如努力学习。"

Translation:

The Master says, "I once spent whole day and night thinking, with no time to eat or sleep. Gaining no profit, I should have used the time on learning."

新 解

有些学生有多思而少学的倾向,其实许多事情光是自己空想是没有用的。孔子从亲身实践中认识到学习要和思考相辅相成。学的过程就是探究各种知识所蕴含的内在规律的过程,思考的过程就是把所学知识进行领悟、消化,从而转化为自己内在涵养的过程。知识是要配合思想的,只有通过学习,多读书,多思考,才能解决实际问题。所以,思而不学不对,学而不思也不对。

Contemporary interpretation:

Some students tend to be excessive in thinking and deficient in learning. They do not know that for most problems thinking without learning will get them nowhere. Based on his personal experience, Confucius teaches us that thinking and learning are interdependent —— neither will go without the other. Learning seeks an understanding of the inherent laws among things, while thinking targets comprehension, digestion, and internalization of the learning. Problems in reality calls for more learning, more reading, and more thinking and a greater marriage among them. Thinking without learning is as wrong as learning without thinking.

16. 子曰:"居,吾语汝。好仁不好学,其蔽也愚;好知不好学,其蔽也荡;好信不好学,其蔽也贼;好直不好学,其蔽也绞;好勇不好学,其蔽也乱;好刚不好学,其蔽也狂。"

今 译

孔子说:"仲由呀!你听说过六种美德,六种弊病吗?"子路回答说:"没有听说过。"孔子说:"坐下来,我告诉你吧!爱好仁德而不爱好学习,它的弊病是容易被人愚弄;爱好聪明而不爱好学习,它的弊病是容易放荡;爱好诚信而不爱好学习,它的弊病是容易受害;爱好正直而不爱好学习,它的弊病是说话尖刻;爱好武勇而不爱好学习,它的弊病是容易闯祸;爱好刚强而不爱好学习,它的弊病是容易狂妄自大。"

Translation:

The Master says, "Zilu, have you heard of the six virtues and their corresponding drawbacks?" Zilu answers, "I have not." The Master says, "Sit down and listen to me. To desire benevolence without learning breeds gullibility. To desire clever knowledge without learning will lead to debauchery. To desire honesty without learning will lead to vulnerability. To desire probity without learning will lead to acrimony. To desire bravery without learning will lead to impetuosity. And to desire fortitude without learning will lead to arrogance."

一、为 学（To Learn）

新 解

仁、知、信、直、勇、刚对于一个人来说，都是美德，但如果不和学习结合起来，就无法明白事理。那么即使有心实践品德，也容易产生流弊。仁虽然好，没有真正学问涵养，就会变成是非不分的老好人，受人愚弄。知虽然好，知识渊博，没有真正学问涵养，就会任性、放荡，"名士风流大不拘"，对自己不检点。信虽然好，没有真正学问涵养，就会过分自信，自己害了自己。直虽然好，没有真正学问涵养，心直口快，没有保留，容易得罪人，办坏事。勇虽然好，没有真正学问涵养，就容易出乱子。刚虽然好，但没有真正学问涵养，刚直不转弯，容易主观任意，狂妄自大。所以这六种个性，本身都不是坏事，但如果没有真正内涵的修养，就会产生愚、荡、贼、绞、乱、狂的流弊，都会变成坏事。所以，我们走在人生的正途上，学习是非常重要的，善于在实践中学习，总结前人和自己的经验教训，提高自己的理性分析能力，使自己知道如何在仁爱的原则下，在具体的环境里加以权变，做出灵活、适度的判断和反应，这才是真正学到家了。

Contemporary interpretation:

Benevolence, wisdom, honesty, probity, bravery and fortitude were no doubt all virtues a person should possess. Yet if uncoupled with learning, they each lead you astray. Without learning, excessive benevolence, though a virtue in itself, will be exploited by others, excessive pride in one's own knowledge will breed salacity, excessive honesty will bring harm to oneself, excessive uprightness will tend to offend, excessive bravery will make troubles, and excessive fortitude will produce arrogance and conceit. Therefore, the six virtues will become demerits if they were not properly moderated. In reality, it is very important for us to learn from our predecessors and to become flexible so as to strategically adapt ourselves to suit concrete and varied circumstances.

17. 孔子曰："生而知之者上也，学而知之者次也；困而学之，又其次也；困而不学，民斯为下矣。"

今 译

孔子说："天生就有知识的人是上等人，经过学习掌握知识的人是次等人；遇到困难而学习的人是又次一等的人；遇到困难还不愿学习的人，那是最下等的人了。"

Translation:

The Master says, "People who are innately knowledgeable are superior to those who become knowledgeable through learning, and people who start learning after they encounter problems are superior to those who hate to learn even after they are bombarded by problems."

一、为 学（To Learn）

新 解

孔子把人的资质分为四等，上等的是生而知之，次等的是学而知之，再次等的是困而学之，最次的是困而不学的。不管是哪种人，都要努力学习。天赋甚高而不学习，也会由神童变为蠢材。就连孔子都承认他自己是学而知之的，所以天资不好不要紧，重要的是坚持学习。

Contemporary interpretation:

Confucius divides people into four aptitudes. Congenital knowledge is superior to learned knowledge, which is superior to forced knowledge. The worst is refusal of knowledge. In the opinion of Confucius, no matter what type a person belongs to, he must learn hard. A prodigy that refuses to learn will eventually become a fool. Even the great sage of Confucius considers himself as a man of acquired learning. What matters is not aptitude, but diligence.

---

18. 卫公孙朝问于子贡曰："仲尼焉学？"子贡曰："文武之道，未坠于地，在人。贤者识其大者，不贤者识其小者，莫不有文武之道焉，夫子焉不学，而亦何常师之有？"

今译

卫国公孙朝向子贡请教说:"仲尼从那里学到这么多知识?"子贡说:"周文王和周武王的正道,没有失传,仍散落在人间。贤德的人能记住它的根本,不贤的人也能记住它的末节,没有地方不存在文王、武王的正道啊!我的老师哪里都可以学习,何必一定要有固定的老师呢?"

Translation:

Duke Sun Zhao of Wei asks Zigong, "Where has your teacher learnt so much knowledge?" Zigong answers, "The way of Sire Wen and Wu of the Zhou Dynasty has not become extinct. It still exists today among the populace. The virtuous know its fundamentals. Even the obscure know its minutia. As the way of Sire Wen and Wu is popular among so many, my teacher can easily find one to learn from. The teacher needs not be the same person all the time, need he?"

新解

孔子善学,只要别人有善言善行,有可取之处,孔子都不拘一格,向他学习,所以孔子能够成为圣人。我们现在总是认为"名师出高徒",一心想拜个名师,或者进个名校,以为这样才能有前途。其实,如果是真正懂得学习的人,从身边人或事就能学到知识,同样能够学有所成。

Contemporary interpretation:

As an adept learner, Confucius learns from the good words and deeds of all by all means, thus becoming a saint. The conventional wisdom that a great student comes from a great teacher leads to the idea that a great future comes only from a master teacher or a prestigious university. In the teaching of Confucius, the real learner accomplishes the process by learning from people and affairs nearby.

二、修 身（Self-Edification）

1. 曾子曰："吾日三省吾身：为人谋而不忠乎？与朋友交而不信乎？传不习乎？"

今 译

曾子说："我每天多次省察自身：替他人谋事是否忠诚？与朋友交往是否守信？传授他们的学业是否熟悉了？"

Translation:

Master Zeng says, "I practice three daily introspections: Am I loyal to those on whose behalf I act, am I trustworthy to friends with whom I interact, am I versed in knowledge which I impart?"

新 解

"三省"是儒家的一种道德修养方法，曾子"三省吾身"

二、修 身（Self-Edification）

的思想实际上是孔子"内省"思想的具体阐述。孔子强调要"为人忠"、事君要"能致其身"，对待工作要"居之无倦，行之以忠"，为别人办事要尽心竭力；结交朋友要"言而有信"，要诚实，反对对待朋友阳奉阴违，表里不一。一个人如果不诚实、不讲信用而只是撒谎欺骗，根本就不会交到真正的朋友。对于学习的知识，我们更要去实践巩固，举一反三，将其真正变成自己的东西。自我反省、自我监督、自我教育，这对于我们个人自身修养的提高有着非常重大的作用。

Contemporary interpretation:

The "three introspections" are the Confucian method for cultivation of the virtuous self. Master Zeng offers an elaboration of this Confucian thought. Confucius teaches loyalty to others, devotion to the monarch, dedication to one's work, and reliability to one's friends. Duplicity and dishonesty attracts no true friends. As for knowledge, one should repeatedly review it and widely apply it to achieve genuine internalization of the knowledge as one's own. Introspection, self-inspection, and self-education are indispensable for cultivation of the virtuous self.

---

2. 子贡曰："贫而无谄，富而无骄，何如？"子曰："可也。未若贫而乐，富而好礼者也。"

论语 今译新解

今 译

子贡说:"贫困而不谄媚,富有而不傲慢,怎么样?"孔子说:"可以啊,但不如贫困而快乐,富有而喜好礼。"

Translation:

Zigong asks, "What about poverty without servility and wealth without superiority?" The Master says, "Good! But better still if he finds joy in poverty or practices civility despite wealth."

新 解

孔子教导子贡,修养不仅是行善,更重要的是乐道。子贡由此悟到了学习要不断深化的道理。古人常说要安贫乐道,贫穷的时候不奉承巴结别人,有钱的时候也不摆出一副颐指气使的派头,要保持心灵的平静,这也是谦谦君子应有的气度。金钱的可怕,就在于当一个人意志薄弱时主宰他的思想,使他丢掉做人的准则。

Contemporary interpretation:

Here Confucius preaches to Zigong about virtue, emphasizing that seeking truth is as important as practicing charity. This dialogue reveals to Zigong the essence of ultimate knowledge. The ancients advocated contentment in poverty, joy in charity, no obsequious servility when poor, and no boastful ostentation when rich. A calm and modest heart shields the person from the corrupting power of money and from the loss of the principle of civility.

3. 子曰:"不患人之不己知,患不知人也。"

今 译

孔子说:"不担心别人不了解我,要担心我不了解别人。"

Translation:

The Master says, "I do not grieve that other people do not recognize my merits, but I grieve that I may well fail to recognize their merits."

新 解

此章告诉人们,遇到问题首先应寻求自身的原因。有些人呼唤"理解万岁",有些人感慨自己"怀才不遇"、"生不逢时",却没有冷静地思考过自己是否同样不了解别人。孔子就是能够站在充分理解别人的角度上来发出感慨,如果别人不了解自己,那是自己做得还不够,如果自己不了解别人,又当如何?我们作为社会的人,不要总是发牢骚、埋怨别人,而是应时时刻刻自我反省,是否忽略了他人的善举。如此一来,人与人之间才会更加相互理解、相互信任。

Contemporary interpretation:

The implication is that when not understood, the person should first search within. The outcry for others' understanding and the lament over "unrecognized talent" and "inauspicious time" all reveal an unawareness of the importance of first understanding others. Confucius edifies from the vantage point of full empathy. If not understood, we are deficient in our deeds. Any thought to our inadequacy in giving understanding? Our membership in the society calls for a refrain from complaining and blaming, but for a constant practice of introspection and gratitude. This may prove the sole road to mutual understanding and trust.

---

4. 子曰:"人而无信,不知其可也。大车无輗,小车无軏,其何以行之哉?"

今 译

孔子说:"做人而不讲信用,不知道他怎么可以立身处世。好像牛车没有安装輗,马车没有安装軏,它怎么能行走呢?"

Translation:

The Master says, "Without an axle, a cart cannot go. False to one's word, a man is not tenable."

新 解

这章中孔子用比喻说明了信的重要性。孔子教导人要讲信用，失去信用，就像车子失去重要的部件而不能行动一样。做人也好，处世也好，为政也好，信是很重要的。说话算数，讲信用，才能取信于人。

Contemporary interpretation:

With this analogy, Confucius illustrates the importance of trust. A man's loss of trust is analogous to a cart's loss of its axle. In self-conduct, in human affairs, or in statecraft, trust is given only to those true to their words.

---

5. 子曰："见贤思齐焉，见不贤而内自省也。"

今 译

孔子说："见到贤人就向他看齐，看见不贤的人，就从内心反省自己。"

Translation:

The Master says, "When we see a good person, we should follow his suit. When we see a bad person, we should practice introspection."

新解

　　个人道德修养的重要原则就是：向贤者学习，与之看齐；以后进为戒，多作自我反省，反思一下自己身上有没有他的毛病。一个善于学习的人，从任何人身上都可以学到有益的东西。好的就是正面教材，坏的就是反面教材，从他们的错误中也可吸取教训。能够如此，天下人个个都是你的老师了，自己的仁德修养又怎么能不提高呢？

Contemporary interpretation:

A virtuous self requires emulation of the good and self-examination against the bad to see whether you suffer similar faults. An adept learner imbibes lessons from both the positive and the negative. As Confucius teaches, everyone else is our teacher. When doing so, how can cultivation of virtue and benevolence be impossible?

---

6. 子曰："质胜文则野，文胜质则史。文质彬彬，然后君子。"

今译

　　孔子说："朴质胜过文采，就显得粗野；文采胜过朴质，

二、修 身 (Self-Edification)

就显得虚浮。既文雅又朴质，结合适当，才算得上是个君子。"

Translation:

The Master says, "When simpleness overshadows culture, provinciality shows. When culture overshadows simpleness, ostentation shows. Cultured simpleness makes a gentleman."

新 解

孔子认为：一个人虽然本性善良质朴，还需要外在的文雅言行配合，才显君子风范。质朴而不粗野，文雅而不虚伪才算是君子。生活中有些人为人朴实善良，但是缺乏修养，让人觉得粗野。另外有些人只会读书，但是没有实际能力，成为百无一用的书呆子。这两种人都不是君子，谦谦君子是既要有内心高贵的品德，又要具备高雅的言行才算完美。"文质彬彬"才是我们努力的方向。

Contemporary interpretation:

In Confucius' opinion, a simple and good-natured person needs to be educated and refined to become a gentleman. A true gentleman should not be so simple as to appear crude or practice refinement such as to become pretentious. He must strike a proper balance between the two. In life, some simple and honest people often leave the others an impression of crudeness due to their lack of manners; whereas some other people, so learned and yet so impractical, are called worthless pedants. Both types of people are no gentlemen. To be a gentleman, one must be inwardly simple and outwardly refined at once. And this must be what we each aim to achieve.

> 7. 子绝四：毋意，毋必，毋固，毋我。

今 译

孔子杜绝四种弊病：不随意猜测，不主观武断，不固执己见，不自以为是。

Translation:

The Master rids himself of four flaws: speculation, dogmatism, obstinacy and self conceit.

新 解

孔子处事不凭主观臆测，不墨守成规，不绝对武断，不自以为是。一个人一生中在行为修养上能够做到这"四绝"，实在非常难。常言说："不如意事常十之八九"，人生的事大多不可能尽如人意，天下事随时在变，我们自身也在变，没有不变的事物。要避免主观、片面，要学会应变，还要"毋我"，就是要替别人着想，不固执己见。

Contemporary interpretation:

In conducting himself, Confucius never speculates

二、修 身（Self-Edification）

groundlessly, nor blindly clings to the rules, nor acts arbitrarily, nor appears self-conceited. Instead, His modesty inclines him to constantly learn from others. Surely it is a feat to wean oneself from the four flaws. As the adage goes, "What displeases outweighs what pleases in worldly life." The inevitable change requires constant adaptation and vigilance against presumption. Practice not egocentrism, but altruism.

8. 子曰："岁寒然后知松柏之后凋也！"

今 译

孔子说："寒冷的冬天，才知道松树、柏树是最后凋谢的。"

Translation:

The Master says, "Only in cold winter do we know the pine is the last to wither."

新 解

这是一句名言。松柏有着顽强的生命力，而且经冬不凋，古人常用松柏来象征高洁的品行，这句话是孔子用来表彰在逆境中意志坚定的君子的。俗话说："路遥知马力，日久见人心。"只有在艰难困苦的条件下，才能考验人的真伪善恶。学习也是这样，学习不可能永远一帆风顺，也要有松柏一样坚韧不拔的精神和毅力。经历了重重考验后，人生就进行了一次次飞跃。

Contemporary interpretation:

This remark has become a celebrated aphorism. The pine, because of its strong vitality in cold winter, is often used to epitomize a person's noble virtues and behavior. The remark later on is often used by people to praise those who are determined and perseverant in adversity. Just as a Chinese saying goes, "As distance tests the horse, so does longevity with a man". Character shows but in adversity. The same is true of learning. So is the journey to knowledge, which is not smooth sailing, but requires pine-like fortitude and tenacity. Miracle comes from repeated victory over adversity.

---

9. 颜渊问仁。子曰："克己复礼为仁。一日克己复礼，天下归仁焉。为仁由己，而由人乎哉？"颜渊曰："请问其目？"子曰："非礼勿视，非礼勿听，非礼勿言，非礼勿动。"

今 译

颜渊问孔子什么是仁。孔子说："克制自己，使言行符合

二、修 身（Self-Edification）

于礼就是仁。一旦言行符合于礼，天下的人都会称许你是仁人了。实行仁完全在自己，难道还靠别人吗？"颜渊说："请问实施仁的细目。"孔子说："不合礼的事不看；不合礼的话不听；不合礼的话不说；不合礼的事不做。"

Translation:

Yanyuan asks the Master what virtue is. The master says, "virtue is to discipline yourself so as to act and to speak in accordance with decorum. So long as you can achieve this, then you become worthy to be named "the virtuous". To practice virtue, you could rely on nobody else but yourself. Yanyuan asks again, "Can you elaborate on the specificities of virtue?" The Master answers, "Look not onto the indecorous. Hear not the indecorous. Say not the indecorous. Practice not the indecorous."

新 解

"仁"是孔子伦理思想的核心，心目中的最高道德标准。孔子认为，约束自身，也就能循礼而行，就可以达到仁的境界。可见，求仁与否完全在于自己而不在于别人。至于非礼"勿视、勿听、勿言、勿动"则是阐明仁与礼的关系，也就是实施仁的内容。只要视、听、言、动都合乎礼，行乎正道，仁的境界也就达到了。

Contemporary interpretation:

Virtue is the core of Confuciunism and the consummation of virtue. In Confucius' opinion, if a person could discipline himself with social decorum, he could reach a higher spiritual status of benevolence. The proper way to discipline oneself is to follow the Confucian four "don'ts" as he said to Yan Yuan.

---

10. 仲弓问仁。子曰:"出门如见大宾,使民如承大祭。己所不欲,勿施于人。在邦无怨,在家无怨。"

今 译

仲弓问孔子什么是仁。孔子说:"出门见人,好像会见贵宾一样,治理百姓,好像承担重大祭祀。自己所不喜欢的东西,不要强加于人。在朝廷做官没有怨恨,在家赋闲也没有怨恨。"

Translation:

Zhong Gong asks the Master about virtue. The Master says, "When you go out to meet someone, treat that person as if he were an important guest. In the same way, ruling a country is like presiding over an important ritual of sacrifice. Do not do unto others what you do not want done unto yourself. And never grudge whether you live in official importance, or in homely obscurity."

新 解

孔子提出三方面实施仁的内容:首先,要对人、对事恭敬和谨慎。不管出门待人接物、管制百姓,都要像接待贵宾,承

二、修 身 (Self-Edification)

办祭祀一样，恭敬谨慎。第二，对人要实行恕道，"己所不欲，勿施于人"，推己及人，这是具有仁人之心的表现。第三，对别人都没有怨恨，自然其他人也不会来怨恨我们。而这三者的核心，就是实行恕道，做到"己所不欲，勿施于人"，它也成为全球道德的"金规则"，被人们广泛接受。

Contemporary interpretation:

Confucius proffers three components of the practice of virtue. Firstly, we should pay much respect for the people around us and treat them the same way as we treat those honored guests and with the same sincerity as we show on occasion of those holy rituals. Secondly, we must be considerate and tolerant, not doing unto others what we do not want done unto ourselves. Empathy is emblem of virtue. And thirdly, do not grudge and you will not receive a grudge. The core of virtue is tolerance. The Confucian teaching of "Do unto others what you want done on yourself" has become a global "golden rule" of behavior.

11. 樊迟问仁。子曰："爱人。"问知。子曰："知人。"樊迟未达。子曰："举直错诸枉，能使枉者直。"樊迟退，见子夏曰："乡也吾见于夫子而问知，子曰：'举直错诸枉，能使枉者直'。何谓也？"子夏曰："富哉，言乎！舜有天下，选于众，举皋陶，不仁者远矣。汤有天下，选于众，举伊尹，不仁者远矣。"

论语 今译新解

今 译

樊迟问孔子,什么是仁。孔子说:"爱别人。"又问知。孔子说:"了解别人。"樊迟没有完全理解。孔子补充说:"选拔正直的人放在邪恶的人上面,能够让邪恶的人变得正直。"樊迟走了出来,遇到子夏。便对子夏说:"刚才我见到老师,请教什么是知,老师说:'选拔正直的人放在邪恶的人上面,能够使邪恶的人变为正直',这是什么意思呢?"子夏说:"这句话的内涵多么深刻呀!舜统治天下,在众人中选拔人才,把皋陶选拔出来,不仁德人就远远地离开了。商汤统治天下,在众人中选拔人才,把伊尹选拔出来,不仁德的人也远远地离开了。"

Translation:

Fan Chi asks Confucius what enquires on virtue. The Master says, "Love your fellows." He asks what knowledge is. The master says, "Know the others around you." Fan Chi does not understand clearly, so the Master adds, "If you choose an upright person to preside over an evil person, the evil person will become upright." Still baffled, Fan Chi consults Zixia, whom he sees on the way out, "Just now I consulted the Master on knowledge and was given the response 'A man of probity, if chosen to preside over a man of depravity, will rectify the latter.' What does it really mean?" Zi Xia answers, "What a rich implication! Take King Shun and King Tang for example. When King Shun ruled the country, he elected Gao Tao from the rabble, at whose sight the non-virtuous flees.

二、修 身（Self-Edification）

When King Tang ruled the state, he elected Yi Yin from the rabble, at whose sight the non-virtuous flees."

新 解

孔子认为仁就是从人性发展出来的博爱、友爱，因此对人要宽恕体谅。另外，孔子认为知是了解人。知人的问题，对统治者来说是至关重要的。舜和汤用人得当，取得施政的成功，桀和纣用人不当，终致灭亡，这些历史的经验教训，都有借鉴意义。

Contemporary interpretation:

Confucius believes that virtue could be understood as universal fraternity and friendship. Therefore, we should practice tolerant empathy onto others. As for knowledge, Confucius emphasizes the importance of knowing the people you employ. He believes that it is very important for the rulers to know well about the person they choose for a position. King Shun and King Tang's successful ruling lies with their proper choice of officers. In contrast, Jie and Zhou's ruined ruling lies with their improper choice of officers. All of these historical experience and lessons are helpful to the governors of the nations today.

---

12. 樊迟问仁。子曰："居处恭，执事敬，与人忠。虽之夷狄，不可弃也。"

今 译

樊迟问什么是仁。孔子说:"平时闲居态度端庄,办事认真严肃,对人忠实诚信。即使到边远的少数民族地方去,也不能丢弃这些品德。"

Translation:

Fan Chi asks the Master about virtue. The Master says, "A person of humanity should be modest in demeanor, serious to his work, and trustful to his friends. Even if he goes to a faraway community, he should not forsake these virtues.

新 解

为人处世必须掌握恭、敬、忠三个原则。恭是对平日自处而言,言行要恭敬而谨慎,保持严肃的态度;敬,是对处事而言,对工作要尽心尽责,切勿马虎草率;忠,是对上级、交友而言,对朋友、对下属都要忠实诚信。这是做人的基本原则。

Contemporary interpretation:

Prudence and modesty are to be exercised in everyday conduct; a conscientious dedication, in work; and trustworthiness, with superiors and friends. This forms the cardinal principle for a man of virtue.

二、修 身（Self-Edification）

13. 子曰："君子泰而不骄，小人骄而不泰。"

今 译

孔子说："君子安详舒坦而不骄气凌人，小人骄气凌人而不安详舒坦。"

Translation:

The Master says, "A gentleman is dignified but not arrogant, whereas an ignoble person is arrogant but not composed."

新 解

孔子从人际关系上对比了君子与小人的不同心态和截然相反的待人方式：君子思想品德修养高，私心少，胸襟开阔，气度宽宏，因而安详舒泰而绝不骄傲。小人思想品德修养差，私心重，患得患失，因而常常局促忧虑，既骄傲，又自卑，不能安详舒泰。

Contemporary interpretation:

Confucius contrasts the noble with the ignoble: the former is cultured, altruistic, magnanimous, and thus achieves modesty and dignity; the latter is uncultured, egoistic, and materialistic, and thus

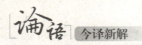

suffers from the indignity of angst, arrogance, diffidence.

14. 子曰:"刚、毅、木、讷近仁。"

今 译

孔子说:"刚强、坚毅、朴质、语言谨慎,具有这四种品德的人接近于仁道了。"

Translation:

The Master says, "A person, if resolute, tenacious, simple, and circumspect, approximates virtue."

新 解

刚毅,属于外向型,具有这种品性的人,正直坚强,不为物欲所屈,能见义勇为。木讷,属于内向型;具有这种品性的人,心地善良,不为利欲所诱而轻举妄动。能够做到刚、毅、木、讷,就是一个办事踏实,备受人们信赖的人。

Contemporary interpretation:

A staunch and perseverant person is usually extroversive, upright and unyielding before material temptation. A simple and prudent person is usually introversive, kind-hearted and will not be

二、修 身（Self-Edification）

swayed by bribery. If a person has all the four qualities mentioned by the Master, he will be regarded as honest and trustworthy.

15. 子曰："君子义以为质，礼以行之，孙以出之，信以成之。君子哉！"

今 译

孔子说："君子用道义作为根本，用礼仪来实行它，用谦逊来表达它，用诚信来完成它。这才是真正的君子呀！"

Translation:

The Master says, "A gentleman chooses righteousness as his first principle. He practices righteousness in etiquette, expresses it in modesty, and fulfills it in integrity. And this produces the true gentleman."

新 解

孔子提出义、礼、逊、信作为君子行为的四条原则：首先是本质上要有义。也就是适宜、合宜，既是应该具备的仁义，也是探求义理，属于君子的内心修养。其次是礼，行动要求循礼而行。其三是逊，即谦逊，说话谦逊恭谨。第四是信，办事守信，取信于人。能够做到这几条，就能够保证不入邪道，还能得到周围人的尊敬。因为你正言正行,礼貌待人,自然就会树敌少。谦虚、诚信使你远佞人,近贵人,能在道德、学问、事业等方面步步高升。

Contemporary interpretation:

Confucius puts forth righteousness, etiquette, modesty and integrity as the four cardinal principles a gentleman should follow. In his opinion, righteousness means being just and appropriate. It reveals a person's inner cultivation. By etiquette, he teaches behavior according to norms of etiquette. By modesty he means that a gentleman should keep a low profile in public. By integrity he means that a gentleman should keep his word and have credit. A person in possession of the four cardinal principles will not go astray and could win respect for himself because these principles will help him estrange those who are mean and befriend those who are noble. The benefit from this is continuous edification and progress in his morality, learning and career.

16. 子曰:"君子求诸己,小人求诸人。"

今 译

孔子说:"君子严格要求自己,小人严格要求别人。"

二、修 身（Self-Edification）

Translation:

The Master says, "A gentleman is rigorous with himself, whereas an ignoble person, with others."

新 解

孔子论述了君子、小人修养品格之不同。孔子总是谆谆教育人们要责己严，待人宽，出了问题，君子是从自身寻找原因。小人则相反，他们宽以待己，严以律人，出了问题就从别人身上找原因。一念之间，即可分出高下。

Contemporary interpretation:

By summarizing their different self cultivations Confucius draws two pictures respectively for the gentlemen and the ignoble persons. According to Confucius, a gentleman should be always strict with himself and tolerant of the others. Only the ignoble persons will shift his blame on the others. A tiny difference in thoughts leads to the dichotomy between "noble" and "ignoble".

17. 子夏曰："小人之过也，必文。"

今 译

子夏说："小人对于错误，一定要加以掩饰。"

Translation:

Zixia says, "The ignoble glosses his flaws with embellishments."

新 解

有些人对于自己的过错,总是想方设法说出一堆理由,把错误掩盖起来。殊不知自欺欺人,会越描越黑,结果就是一错再错,难以挽回。不善于改正自己错误的人又怎么可能取得成绩呢?孔子说过:"过则勿惮改",所以要知错就改,不要文过饰非。

Contemporary interpretation:

Some people tend to find various excuses to cover up their mistakes. They do not know that their lame excuses will only lead to further blunders, irretrievably leading them on the hill of self-deception and denigration. A person who is not good at learning from his mistakes will make no progress at any respect in his life. Remember Confucius's words, "Do not be afraid to correct your mistakes." So do not embellish or disguise but own and correct your mistakes.

---

18. 子夏曰:"君子有三变:望之俨然,即之也温,听其言也厉。"

二、修 身（Self-Edification）

今 译

子夏说："君子有三种变化，望着他，觉得很庄重；接近他，觉得很和蔼；听他说话，觉得很严厉。"

Translation:

Zixia says, "A gentlemen has three faces: serious when looked from afar, amiable when to be with, and meticulous when listened to."

新 解

子夏认为一个有修养的君子，远远望去，其容貌好像很庄重严肃。等到接近他的时候，又觉得很温和可亲，充满了感情。听他说话，却又严厉不苟。这就是君子的风格，也是孔子的风格。

Contemporary interpretation:

Zixia maintains that a person of ideal cultivation should possess the three "faces" as mentioned above. The statement portrays the style of a gentleman as well as that of Confucius.

19. 子贡曰："君子之过也，如日月之食焉：过也人皆见之，更也人皆仰之。"

今 译

子贡说:"君子的错误,好像日食和月食一样;他的错误,人们都能看见;他改正错误,人们都仰望着他。"

Translation:

Zigong says, "A gentleman's mistake, like the solar or lunar eclipse, is visible to all. Once he corrects it, he is revered by all."

新 解

这里子贡论述了君子知错必改的坦诚胸怀和对待过失应持的态度。第一,不怕有过失,不文饰错误,错了就光明正大地承认,立即改正,胸怀坦荡,这样就是君子。第二,"人无完人",谁会没有过错呢?有错就改,像日月一样,不会影响自己的声望,仍像日月一样闪闪发光,为人们所景仰。这种胸襟,自然会得到别人的赞扬。

Contemporary interpretation:

Here Zigong addresses a gentleman's attitude toward his own mistakes. First, when he has made a mistake, he should not cover it up. Instead, he should be open-minded and bravely admit his mistake and correct himself right away. Second, no one is perfect. Mistakes are like the eclipses of the sun and the moon. So long as they are put right immediately, they will not bring about harm to a person's reputation just as the eclipses will not decrease the sun

二、修 身（Self-Edification）

and the moon's luster. A person with such an open mind is sure to be respected.

20. 子曰："躬自厚而薄责于人，则远怨矣。"

今 译

孔子说："责备自己多而责备别人少，就可以远离怨恨了。"

Translation:

The Master says, "If a person is quick to blame the self and slow to blame the others, he is then held in no grudge.

新 解

严于律己，宽以待人是高贵的品德，要想处理好人与人之间的关系，这句话非常重要。孔子要求人们遇事多反省自己，严格要求自己，对别人则要宽容诚心，人际关系自然能够和谐融洽。

Contemporary interpretation:

It is very important to be strict with oneself and lenient with others. At present, this principle is particularly important in building a harmonious society. In Confucius' opinion, we should do much self-examination and always harbor a tolerant heart. Only in this way can we live in peace and harmony.

21. 子曰:"君子谋道不谋食。耕也,馁在其中矣;学也,禄在其中矣。君子忧道不忧贫。"

今 译

孔子说:"君子谋求大道而不谋求衣食。耕田,温饱就在其中了;学习,俸禄就在其中了。所以君子担心大道而不担心贫穷。"

Translation:

The Master says, "A gentleman seeks the Way of truth, not mere livelihood. He engages in farming and thus suffers no hunger. He engages in learning and thus is awarded a salaried office. So a gentleman worries about the Way instead of poverty."

新 解

"忧道不忧贫"的思想对古代知识分子的人生追求影响深远。孔子说:真正有学问的人,以天下为己任的君子,担忧的是能否获得道,而不担心生活的问题。也就是说有真本领的人不怕没有前途,不怕埋没。如果过于急功近利,有时反而会适

二、修 身 (Self-Edification)

得其反。

Contemporary interpretation:

The idea of fearing not poverty but not achieving the Way of truth had deep influence on the life philosophy of ancient scholars. According to Confucian teaching, the true scholar equates the nation's responsibility with his own, fearing not a failure in livelihood, but failure in achieving the Way. That is to say, a person of great ambition and capability need not be worried about his fame or prosperity. Hurrying success may thwart the progress toward it.

三、仁 道（The Way to Virtue）

1. 子曰："不仁者不可以久处约，不可以长处乐。仁者安仁，知者利仁。"

今 译

孔子说："没有仁德的人，不能长久地处在贫困之中，也不可以长久地处在安乐之中。通达仁的境界的人，才愿安住于仁的心境。有智慧的人，才懂得运用智慧，才能发挥仁的妙用。"

Translation:

The Master says, "A person without virtue cannot for long endure adversity or enjoy prosperity. Only those who have understood the essence of virtue know how to use their wisdom and exert the power of virtue."

三、仁　道（The Way to Virtue）

新　解

　　这一章说明仁是安身立命的最佳选择。有了仁，就能素贫贱，安于贫贱，素富贵，行乎富贵，安之若素。而不仁的人以"小我"为中心，向外索求无度，所以难以长期过着简单朴素的生活。贫困待不住，快乐也不会长久。所以，不管面对顺境还是逆境，都能让自己生活在平静、清净的心境中，这就是智慧。人既要融入生活，又要懂得超脱生活，才能使内心保持宁静，这就是人生的智慧。

Contemporary interpretation:

　　This statement indicates that virtue gives a haven to the body and an anchorage to the soul. Poor or rich, a person of virtue is blessed with equanimity. Absent of virtue, life centers on an insatiable and petty self, which finds an austere life impossible. Wisdom embraces and yet transcends the mundane life, finding enduring joy from equability in both austerity and luxury, in both adversity and prosperity.

　　2. 子曰："唯仁者能好人，能恶人。"

今　译

　　孔子说："只有有仁德的人，才能正确地喜爱人，才能正

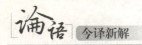

确地去厌恶人。"

Translation:

The Master says, "Only those with virtue can like and dislike the others fairly."

新　解

普通人的好、恶都从小我、私利出发。仁者则不同，其心中坦荡无私，站在公正的立场上，所以能明善辨恶。所以说，仁是判断是非的标准。

Contemporary interpretation:

The ordinary like and dislike according to their self-interest. Virtue does so according to equity. Altruistic and magnanimous, the humane benevolence arbitrates between the kind and the evil, between the true and the false.

3. 子曰："苟志于仁矣，无恶也。"

今　译

孔子说："如果立志实行仁德，就不会憎恶他人了。"

三、仁 道 (The Way to Virtue)

Translation:

The Master says, "If intent on practicing virtue, one grudges against none."

新 解

一个真有了仁的修养的人，对于善人固然能爱他，对于坏人，也能从爱护之心出发，设法拯救他、感化他、改变他，使之改恶从善。仁可以消除邪恶。所以，一个真正有志于仁的人，心中根本不存在敌人，大家平等亲仁，何来仇恨与敌对？

Contemporary interpretation:

A person who has cultivated virtue will no doubt love the virtuous. He even loves the wicked by reforming and converting them into the good. Thus, virtue nullifies evil. A real aspirant for virtue is kind and equitable and hence attracts no enmity.

---

4. 子曰："知者乐水，仁者乐山；知者动，仁者静；知者乐，仁者寿。"

今 译

孔子说："聪明的人喜爱水，仁德的人喜爱山。聪明的人活跃，仁德的人安静。聪明的人快乐，仁德的人长寿。"

Translation:

The Master says, "A wise person delights in water, but a virtuous person in mountains. The wise person is active, but the virtuous person halcyon. The wise is blessed with jocundity and the virtuous, with longevity."

新 解

孔子剖析智者和仁者在性格上的区别十分深刻。智者通达事理,爱好川流不息的水,因而喜动,其结果必然胸襟洒脱,所以多乐。仁者安于义理,少思寡欲,爱好厚重不移的山,其结果必然淡泊寡欲,所以长寿。人的一生中如果能兼得仁智之乐和仁智之长,那就算得上是人生的最高境界了。

Contemporary interpretation:

The Confucian distinction between the dispositions of wisdom and virtue is trenchant. A wise person, flexible and light-hearted, usually loves rivers and sports. Therefore, he has an open mind and enjoys much happiness. A virtuous person, reasonable and tranquil, usually prefers the tranquil mountains. Therefore, he has a peaceful heart and lives long. If a person could combine the advantages of both types, he will reach the acme of virtue.

三、仁 道（The Way to Virtue）

5. 子贡曰："如有博施于民而能济众，何如？可谓仁乎？"子曰："何事于仁，必也圣乎！尧、舜其犹病诸！夫仁者，己欲立而立人；己欲达而达人。能近取譬，可谓仁之方也已。"

今 译

子贡说："如果有人广泛地施恩于人民而且能够救济大众，怎么样？这样的人可以说是仁人了吗？"孔子说："何止仁人！一定是圣人了！尧舜大概还担心做不到呀！有仁德的人，自己站得住脚，也要帮助别人站得住脚，自己想达到的，也要帮助别人能达到。能够推己及人，可以说是实行仁德的方法了。"

Translation:

Zigong asks, "What do you think of someone who can help a great number of people and someone who offers charity to the populace? Is this an act of benevolence?" The Master says, "This person surpasses benevolence and is already a saint, eclipsing even King Yao and King Shun. A benevolent person extends his own success to others. Projection of one's own heart into that of others is the gateway into benevolence."

新 解

本章孔子教子贡就近取仁德的方法。第一，孔子提出心目中的最高道德标准是圣，其次才是仁，两者又是相通的，积仁可以至圣。第二,仁的标准就是"己欲立而立人,己欲达而达人",能做到推己及人,就达到了仁的标准。第三,行恕道乃是为仁的方法,能近取譬,将心比心。孔子也是在委婉地劝告子贡不要好高骛远,要从身边的小事做起,一步步地去做,找到切实可行的行"仁之方"。

Contemporary interpretation:

In this statement Confucius teaches Zigong how to practice benevolence. In Confucius's opinion, the supreme criterion for virtue should be holiness rather than benevolence. Holiness and benevolence is compatible. Accumulation of benevolence may lead to saintliness. The criterion for benevolence is to follow the principle "Help the others make it first". Second, the principle of benevolence teaches that once achieving your standing, help others do the same; once arriving at your destination, help others do the same. Empathy is the hallmark of benevolence. Tolerance may be the third approach toward humane benevolence. Here, Confucius euphemistically advises Zigong against pipe dreams. The Way to benevolence originates with the small steps of doing little things nearby.

6. 子曰:"仁远乎哉?我欲仁,斯仁至矣。"

三、仁 道（The Way to Virtue）

今 译

孔子说："仁离开我们很远吗？我想要仁，仁就来到了。"

Translation:

The Master says, "Is virtue far from us? It comes whenever beckoned."

新 解

仁并不是摸不着、看不到、高不可攀的，求仁并不难，关键问题在于肯不肯求，诚不诚心。仁德的修养只在于人们自身的主观努力，只要肯下功夫，从一点一滴做起，人人都可以求仁而得仁。心中有仁，仁就不远；心中无仁，仁就在九霄云外。

Contemporary interpretation:

Virtue is not intangible, invisible, or inaccessible. Its acquisition may not be difficult, yet the secret is whether the pursuit is earnest. Virtue blesses any willing intent and any patient effort. Once in your heart, it is in your hand. If not in your heart, it is beyond heaven's reach.

7. 子曰："人之过也，各于其党。观过，斯知仁矣。"

今 译

孔子说:"人们的错误就在周围的人和事中。省察这些过错,就了解仁的内涵了。"

Translation:

The Master says, "All your mistakes reside among those in your company. Observe them and you'll know virtue."

新 解

其实,在生活中人们只要细心观察周围人所犯的错误,就能清楚地知道哪些是错的。那么自己就要反省,自己是不是有同样的过错。假如有,就改过来;假如没有,就更加努力,慢慢就能使自己避免犯这样的错误,从而接近仁的品德。

Contemporary interpretation:

Careful observation of others reveals to you what is wrong. Introspect yourself to see if you suffer similar mistakes as committed by others. If yes, correct them. If no, continue to avert them. You will then be near the gate into virtue.

---

8. 子曰:"好勇疾贫,乱也;人而不仁,疾之已甚,乱也。"

三、仁 道（The Way to Virtue）

今 译

孔子说："喜欢勇武而厌恶贫穷，这是产生祸乱的根源。对于不仁的人，厌恶他们太过分了，也会导致祸乱。"

Translation:

The Master says, "Emulating the valiant and detesting the poor are the curse of unrest. Excess abhorrence against those who are without virtue may incur insurgence as well."

新 解

孔子分析导致社会不安定的原因是：一是喜欢勇武而不安于贫困的人，当生活发生困难时就会铤而走险，发动叛乱。二是对不仁的人，都没有同情心，不能包容，逼得他们无处容身，失去信心，将会产生逆反心理，导致暴乱。如何解决这些问题呢？必须对他们加强教育，提高他们的道德品质修养，让他们自觉地用礼来约束自己。这是一个长期的工程，江山易改，本性难移，碰到这些"好勇疾贫，人而不仁"的人，不要操之过急，保持一颗平常心就行。

Contemporary interpretation:

In this statement Confucius analyzes two causes of social turmoil: One, emulators of the valiant and scorners of the poor may become reckless daredevils when in poverty and stage insurgence. Two, intolerance against those who are without virtue may corner them into such misled animus as to stage insurrection. The solution is patient education and cultivation of their moral character so that they may eventually discipline themselves accordingly. This project of changing the obdurate certainly requires an equable patience.

---

9. 子曰:"知者不惑,仁者不忧,勇者不惧。"

今 译

孔子说:"聪明的人不会疑惑,仁德的人没有忧愁,勇敢的人无所畏惧。"

Translation:

The Master says, "A wise person knows no perplexity; a virtuous person knows no worry; a brave person knows no fear."

新 解

一个人要达成完美的人格修养,必须具备智慧、仁爱、勇敢三种品格。有了这些品格,就能在艰难困苦的逆境中,在瞬息万变的形势中,不惑、不忧、不惧,卓然屹立于天地之间。

Contemporary interpretation:

The consummate character is built upon the three virtues:

三、仁 道（The Way to Virtue）

wisdom, virtue, and bravery. These virtues furnish freedom from confusion, anxiety, and trepidation and implant one against harsh adversity and incessant change.

---

10. 子夏曰："博学而笃志，切问而近思，仁在其中矣。"

今 译

子夏说："广泛地学习，坚守自己的志向，以切己之事问于人，善于思考现实的问题，仁德就在其中了。"

Translation:

Zixia says, "Virtue resides in extension of knowledge and intensification of the aim, and in earnest enquiry and contemplation of the earthly mundane."

新 解

从身边事出发，通过学习、思考、巩固，就可以修养仁德。仁，看起来好像是抽象的，其实就在你的身边。那就是要"切问而近思"。切问就是经验，就是要多听多问。有了经验后，还要近思，要真正有思想，由身边的事去思索，去体会人生经验。

Contemporary interpretation:

Virtue could be fostered by learning, thinking and consolidating. Seemingly elusive, virtue concerns so much that is so close to us. Real virtue applies earnest enquiry and thinking toward real issues in everyday life.

---

11. 子张问仁于孔子。孔子曰:"能行五者于天下为仁矣。"请问之。曰:"恭、宽、信、敏、惠。恭则不侮,宽则得众,信则人任焉,敏则有功,惠则足以使人。"

今 译

子张问孔子怎样才是仁。孔子说:"能实行五种品德,就算是仁了。"子张问是哪五种。孔子说:"恭敬、宽容、诚信、勤敏、慈惠。恭敬就不会招致侮辱,宽容就能得到众人的拥护,诚信就能得到别人的任用,勤敏就能取得成功,慈惠就可以使唤人。"

Translation:

Zizhang asks Confucius about virtue. Confucius says, "Virtue practices five qualities." Zizhang further asks. Confucius says, "The five qualities include reverence, leniency, honesty, industry and

三、仁 道（The Way to Virtue）

kindness. Reverence averts humiliation; leniency gives popularity; honesty brings office; industry produces success; and kindness entices compliance."

新 解

行仁不能离开做人做事的表现。走在人生征途上，要处理好人与人之间的关系。第一，对人要谦恭，从内心思想到外表行动都要严肃，恭谨。第二，对人宽宏大量，能包容部下朋友的短处和小过失。第三，要信任人，你信任别人，人家自然也就会用同等的信任来回报你。第四，反应敏捷，能够及时、准确地处理问题，化矛盾于无形，这就是莫大的功劳啊！第五，能够发自内心地帮助别人，自然能赢得别人发自内心的尊重。"恭、宽、信、敏、惠"也就是"仁"在为人处世上的具体体现。

Contemporary interpretation:

In your interactions with others, possession of virtue cannot be separated from its practice. First, be humble with others and be scrupulous in your attitude. Second, be magnanimous and tolerant of others' foibles. Third, trust and you will be requited with trust. Fourth, be perspicacious to thwart the conflict in its bud. A feat it sure is! Fifth, be sincere in charity and you win genuine gratitude. Therefore, practicing the five qualities of reverence, leniency, honesty, industry and kindness is to practice virtue.

12. 子曰:"巧言令色,鲜矣仁!"

今 译

孔子说:"满口说着花言巧语,满脸装着和善的样子讨好别人,这样的人几乎就不具备'仁'的品德"。

Translation:

The Master says, "Glib words and alluring smiles hardly go with virtue."

新 解

"巧言令色"这是一副伪君子的画像。这种人时时刻刻都在讨别人的欢心,他们的言语之中能有几分诚意呢?孔子对伪君子的鄙弃之情溢于言表。这一句话告诫人们不要只看外表,要注重内在的品德修养,要以诚待人,敢于正视自我,承认自我,对别人少一点防御,多一点接受。这样做,你会感到生活是轻松、坦荡、美丽的。

Contemporary interpretation:

Fine words and pretentious smiles are what a hypocrite is good at. Such type of people loses no opportunity to ingratiate themselves with the others. There is little sincerity in their manners. This statement reveals Confucius' effusive disgust for hypocrites. It advises us against judging people only by

三、仁 道（The Way to Virtue）

their appearances. when judging a person, we should pay more attention to his virtues and self-cultivation. Only when you are frank and candid to yourself and to the others can you live a life of ease, candor, and beauty.

13. 子曰："里仁为美。择不处仁，焉得知？"

今 译

孔子说："居住的地方有仁义风尚才是好地方，把居住地选择在没有仁义的地方，怎么能算明智呢？"

Translation:

The Master says, "It is the vogue of virtue that gives to a neighborhood its attraction. A person choosing his dwelling in a place lacking in virtue could not be accorded the name of the wise."

新 解

荀子说："蓬生麻中，不扶而直，白沙在涅，与之俱黑。"可见，环境对人的重要影响。选择有仁德的地方居住，为培养人创造好的条件，这是智者的做法。我们为学，也要有落实的地方，要以仁为标准，达到仁的境界，这才是智慧。

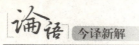

Contemporary interpretation:

Master Xun says, "Fleabanes surrounded by hemps grow upright; white sands mired in alunite become black." It tells us that living environment is very important to a person's growth. A wise person should choose an ideal place to live in, and to choose good neighbors to live with. To obtain virtue, a person should make friends with those who are virtuous and dwell in the place where virtue has been set up as a custom. This is what a wise person will do.

四、礼 乐（Ritual and Music）

> 1. 有子曰："礼之用，和为贵。先王之道斯为美，小大由之。有所不行，知和而和，不以礼节之，亦不可行也。"

今 译

有子说："礼在应用的时候，以创造和谐最为可贵。古代帝王的治国原则，就以这一点最为完美，无论大事小事都要依循礼的规定。遇到有些地方行不通时，如果只知为了和谐而求和谐，没有以礼来节制的话，恐怕还是成不了事的。"

Translation:

You Ruo says, "Etiquette aspires to harmony. Ancestral emperors found perfection in their statecraft that was endorsed by rites of etiquette. Harmony at the cost of etiquette is feckless."

新 解

"礼"是《论语》里一个很重要的概念。礼就是要把人与人之间的关系调节到合适的程度,也就是人与人之间的正常秩序。总结尧舜到周武王时代的政治,最宝贵的就在于"和为贵"。人和天下宁,人心和顺,人与人之间的关系就会融洽,家庭就会温暖,民族就能团结,国家才能欣欣向荣。但是创造"和谐",并不是为了和而和,如果凡事只当和事佬,对矛盾双方不分青红皂白各打五十大板,表面维护一团和气的假象,不以"礼"来约束人们的行为,也是行不通的。

Contemporary interpretation:

Etiquette is a very important concept in *The Analects*. The purpose of etiquette is to regulate the relationships among people to an optimum degree. If we summarize the governing experience of Emperors Yao, Shun and Wu, we could see that their most successful experience is "harmony". When harmony prevails, the populace will be blessed with peace; the family, warmth; the races, fellowship; and the nation, prosperity. However, harmony must be guided by etiquette. Harmony for its own sake produces a false façade of peace and complaisance and eventually leads to inequitable punishment.

2. 子曰:"人而不仁,如礼何? 人而不仁,如乐何?"

四、礼 乐（Ritual and Music）

今 译

孔子说："做人却不讲仁德，礼仪对他有什么意义呢？做人却不讲仁德，音乐对他有什么意义呢？"

Translation:

The Master says, "A person without virtue benefits neither from etiquette nor from music."

新 解

孔子认为仁是礼乐的根本，不仁的人，不能行礼乐。其实，仁与礼的关系是十分密切的，礼的本质是教人尊老爱幼，培养自己的美德，可以看成是仁的精神具体化、外在化。一个人如果本质是坏的，只有彬彬有礼的外表，仍然是一个令人憎恶的伪君子。所以仁是最为基础的品质。

Contemporary interpretation:

Confucius thinks that virtue is the basis of etiquette and music. In his opinion, a person without virtue will not practice etiquette and enjoy music. This is because that the relationship between virtue and etiquette is very close. The essence of etiquette is to teach people to respect the old and love the young. So we can see that etiquette actually is the materialization and externalization of virtue. A person, if evil in nature, remains a repugnant hypocrite despite a polite appearance. Therefore, virtue is the most important

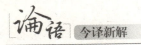

thing a person should possess.

---

3. 林放问礼之本。子曰："大哉问！礼，与其奢也，宁俭；丧，与其易也，宁戚。"

今 译

林放请教礼的根本道理。孔子说："你提的真是个大问题！一般的礼，与其铺张奢侈，宁可俭约朴素；至于丧礼，与其仪式周全，不如心中哀戚。"

Translation:

Lin Fang asks the Master about the quintessence of the ritual. The Master says, "A big question it sure is! Rituals generally favor frugality over extravagance. As for the mourning-rites, sincere lament is better than grand ceremony."

新 解

孔子认为：礼是反映人内在情感、美德的，不是做给别人看的，礼不必铺张浪费用以炫耀，节俭就好。孔子的这种主张对现代社会的一些不正之风也是有力地针砭。中国人逢年过节喜欢送礼，这只是用来表示对亲戚朋友的问候之情的，不是用来炫耀财富和地位，更不是用来攀比的。俗话说：礼轻情意重。

四、礼 乐（Ritual and Music）

只要表示了自己的心意就好，并不一定是越贵重就表示心越诚。时下，送礼的攀比之风已经让好多人害怕送礼，送不起礼，甚至有人打肿脸充胖子，靠借债去送礼，这就是根本歪曲了礼的精神和本意，只能表现出人心的虚荣和肤浅。

Contemporary interpretation:

In Confucius' opinion, etiquette is a reflection of a person's inner feelings and virtues. It is not practiced for show. So in a specific ceremony, frugality should be encouraged and extravagance should not. This Confucian teaching mortifies the unhealthy social practices in our society. To gift in celebratory occasions is a Chinese habit. It is to express the goodwill and the good wish, not to flaunt one's status and wealth or to compete with the Jones. Just as the saying goes, "The gift, though of little account, says my goodwill profound". The essence of a gift resides in its sincerity, not in its size. Nowadays, the unhealthy competition in giving expensive presents has led to the anomaly of "gifting on debts" and has daunted many from attending their friends' celebratory occasions. Such practice distorts the spirit and intention of etiquette and shows nothing but vanity and vacuity.

4. 子曰："礼云礼云，玉帛云乎哉？乐云乐云，钟鼓云乎哉？"

论语 今译新解

今 译

孔子说:"我们说礼啊礼啊,难道只是在说玉帛这些礼品吗?我们说乐啊乐啊,难道只是在说这些乐器吗?"

Translation:

The Master says, "Etiquette, oh etiquette, is it not more than jade and silk? Music, oh music, is it not more than bells and drums?"

新 解

礼有具体表现的形式与器物,但是更重要的却是行礼之人的真实情感。送给别人一些礼物难道就是懂礼吗?知道乐器的知识就是懂得音乐吗?只有领悟到礼、乐背后的精神才能真正活学活用。礼乐的精神要传达真、善、美的情感,否则就徒具形式。

Contemporary interpretation:

There is no denying that any ritual has its specific practices and any present has its substantial form. But what matters is the sincere feelings and emotions of the person who gives the present or perform the ritual. Giving presents to the others does not indicate that one understands the essential meaning of etiquette. The essence of etiquette may not lie in the act of gifting; nor the essence of music, in the knowledge of instruments. Only when a

四、礼 乐（Ritual and Music）

person has really understood the spirit related to the etiquette and music can he truly perform the ritual and appreciate the music. The purpose of ritual and music is to communicate emotions of the true, the good, and the beautiful. Otherwise, it is a mere meaningless form.

5. 陈亢问于伯鱼曰："子亦有异闻乎？"对曰："未也。尝独立，鲤趋而过庭，曰：'学《诗》乎？'对曰：'未也。''不学《诗》，无以言。'鲤退而学《诗》。他日又独立，鲤趋而过庭，曰：'学《礼》乎？'对曰：'未也''不学《礼》，无以立。'鲤退而学《礼》。闻斯二者。"陈亢退而喜曰："问一得三，闻《诗》，闻《礼》，又闻君子之远其子也。"

今 译

陈亢请教伯鱼（孔子的儿子）说："您在老师那儿听过不同的教诲吗？"伯鱼回答说："没有。他曾经一个人站在堂上，我恭敬地从庭前走过，他问：'学《诗》了吗？'我答：'没有。'他说：'不学《诗》，就没有说话的凭借。'我就马上去学诗。另外一天，他又一个人站在堂上，我恭敬地从庭前走过，他问：'学礼了吗？'我答：'没有。'他说：'不学《礼》，就没有立身处世的凭借。'我马上去学《礼》。我听到的是这两件事。"陈亢回去以后,高兴地说:"我问一件事,却知道了三件事:知道要学《诗》,知道要学《礼》,又知道君子不偏爱自己的儿子。"

Translation:

Chen Kang asks Boyu, son of the Master, "Have you had any different instructions from our teacher?" Boyu answers, "No. One day he was standing in the front of the classroom and I reverently advanced toward him. He asked me, 'Have you learned by heart the *Book of Songs?*' I answered, 'Not yet.' He said, 'You will not speak elegantly if you do not memorize the *Book of Songs*.' Then I left and spend much time learning poems from the book. On another day he was standing in the front of the classroom and I reverently advanced toward him again. He asked me, 'Have you learned the *Record of Rites?*' I answered, 'Not yet.' He said, "You will not become established if you do not know the *Record of Rites*." Then I left and spend much time learning etiquette from the book. That is all I have got from him. Chen Kang gladly went back, saying to the others, "I asked Boyu about one thing and I learned three. Now I know, as a gentleman, one must learn poems and etiquette, and one should not be partial to his son."

新 解

这是孔子教子的很生动的一章,按陈亢的说法,可以从中学到三件事。一是学《诗》以言的道理。春秋时期,人们通过赋《诗经》中的诗句来委婉地表达自己的想法和意志,可以说《诗经》是上流人士在重大的外交场合运用的外交语言。现在《诗经》

四、礼 乐（Ritual and Music）

当然没有那么大的功用了，但是学些诗歌能够增长见闻，使人言谈文雅当然是有好处的。二是学礼以立的道理。掌握必备的礼仪知识，就能在社会的各种场合和各种社交活动中，使自己的言行举止合乎礼制规范，能够获得别人的尊重和接纳。三是君子对待自己孩子的态度。孔子对自己儿子的教育和对待学生的教育一样，没有偏爱。这种不私其子的正派作风也是很不容易做到的。

Contemporary interpretation:

This statement vividly reveals Confucius' selflessness and impartiality in teaching his disciples. We could learn three things from this passage. First, learn from the *Book of Songs* to speak well. During the Spring and Autumn Period, people used poems from the *Book* to give deft and subtle expressions of themselves. Dignitaries sought apt quotations from the *Book* for diplomatic occasions. Second, learn the etiquette for social foothold. Knowledge of the rites configures our speech and acts in accordance with sanctioned norms in society and thus wins us acceptance and respect. Third, emulate Confucius and equally treat every person. This is particularly important to teachers and high-ranking officials.

6. 子曰："君子博学于文，约之以礼，亦可以弗畔矣夫！"

今译

孔子说:"有志于成为君子的人,广泛学习文献知识,再以礼来约束自己的行为,这样也就不至于背离人生正途了。"

Translation:

The Master says, "Whoever aspires to be a gentleman learns from recorded knowledge and guides his behaviors with etiquette. This way he will not deviate from the right way to life."

新解

怎样才能不违背仁道呢?孔子教人一是要博学。也就是要多学习,陶冶情操,提高自身的道德修养。二是要用礼制来约束自己。所以博学于文和约之以礼是辩证统一的关系,博学与礼要兼备才能不入歧途。现代教育偏重于博学,而对于礼的重视不够,这样培养出许多虽然文化水平很高,但是人文素养匮乏的人,出现许多高学历罪犯,这不能不说是我们对于礼的教育的缺失。

Contemporary interpretation:

How to avoid deviation from humanity? Confucius teaches two ways: broad knowledge and disciplined decorum. The dialectical unity between the two is the only assurance against deviation from the Way. Modern education stresses knowledge acquisition over etiquette cultivation, producing many high-

四、礼 乐（Ritual and Music）

degreed malefactors, and evincing its own failure.

7. 子曰："恭而无礼则劳，慎而无礼则葸，勇而无礼则乱，直而无礼则绞。君子笃于亲，则民兴于仁；故旧不遗，则民不偷。"

今 译

孔子说："一味谦恭而没有礼的节制，就会流于劳倦；一味谨慎而没有礼的节制，就会显得畏缩；只知勇敢行事而没有礼的节制，就会制造乱局；只知直言无隐而没有礼的节制，就会尖刻伤人。政治领袖对待亲族厚道，百姓就会渐渐走上人生正途；他们不遗弃过去的友人，百姓就不会刻薄无情。"

Translation:

The Master says, "Without the discipline of etiquette, excess modesty engenders indolence; prudence, cowardice; valor, turmoil; and candor, acrimony. Amity to compatriots guides the populace onto the right way. Attention to old friends keeps the populace from malice."

新 解

这里指出人的行为必须受礼法的制约，要掌握分寸。太过于恭敬、谨慎的人，会给人感觉有点假，和他相处也会觉得太累。太过于勇敢直率的人，言行粗鄙，就容易冒犯别人。所以礼的运用要恰到好处。如果领导者能够以身作则，人人都讲究礼仪，言行举止符合一定的社会文明规范，无论在社会生活中还是在社会交际中都表现出应有的教养，那么整个社会风气就会趋于仁爱、和谐。

Contemporary interpretation:

In this statement Confucius emphasizes the importance of "the rules of propriety". In real life, we must properly temper our behaviors in our interactions with others and try not to go to the extremes. This is also applicable to performing etiquette and managing personnel. If the leaders could lead by example, and all the social members could practice etiquette with propriety, there is no doubt that the society will be full of warmth, humanity and harmony.

五、理　想（Ideals）

1. 颜渊、子路侍。子曰："盍各言尔志。"子路曰："愿车马衣轻裘，与朋友共，敝之而无憾。"颜渊曰："愿无伐善，无施劳。"子路曰："愿闻子之志。"子曰："老者安之，朋友信之，少者怀之。"

今　译

颜渊与子路站在孔子身边。孔子说："你们何不说说自己的志向？"子路说："我希望做到：把自己的车子、马匹、衣服、棉袍，与朋友一起用坏了都没有一点遗憾。"颜渊说："我希望做到：不夸耀自己的优点，不把劳苦的事推给别人。"子路说："希望听到老师的志向。"孔子说："使老年人都得到安养，使朋友们都互相信赖，使青少年都得到照顾。"

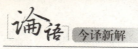

Translation:

The Master says to Yanyuan and Zilu, who are standing next to him, "Tell me about your ambition." Zilu replies, "I would like to share my carriage and my clothing with my friends. I will not regret even if overuse wears them all out." Yanyuan replies, "I hope I can refrain from boasting about my strengths, and from shifting the laborious work to others." Zilu says in relay, "Master, we would like to hear about your ambition." The Master says, "I would like to have the aged well attended, the young well cherished, and the hearts of people frankly communicated."

新 解

本章中师生各自言志,表现各自的性格,展示了不同的胸襟。子路侠义豪放,胸襟开阔,他的理想是重义轻财,颜渊性格谦和,涵养深厚,他表现了仁人之志,孔子则更高一层,以"仁者爱人"的胸襟,展现了对以爱天下为己任,平治天下的抱负。对老年人,物质上、精神上都有所安顿;朋友之间,互相信任,没有仇恨,没有怀疑;对少年,关心培养,爱护他们,这是一种希望天下大同的圣人之志。三个人的精神境界不同,所以理想也各有不同。不管如何,三人的理想之中都有值得我们学习效仿的地方。

Contemporary interpretation:

Different people have different ambitions. Either Zilu's emphasis on friendship, or Yanyuan's emphasis on modesty, or Confucius' emphasis on social responsibility, each is a positive and praise-worthy ambition, and each has something for us to learn from.

五、理　想（Ideals）

> 2. 子曰："三军可夺帅也，匹夫不可夺志也。"

今　译

三军的统帅可能被劫走，一个平凡人的志向却不能被改变。

Translation:

The Master says, "You may rob the Three Armies of their commander-in-chief, but you cannot deprive the humblest person of his ambition."

新　解

三军的力量是强大的，匹夫与三军相比，力量是微乎其微。但是匹夫的理想一旦确立，便有了坚定而崇高的理想和气节。可见立志的重要性。孔子教育年轻人要立下大志，更要落到实处，要有恪守信念的坚定意志，坚持不懈，时刻反省、督促自己，以达到至善至美的境地。

Contemporary interpretation:

The power of the Three Armies is very great. Compared with it, the power of a person is very little. True as it is, so long as a person has set an ambition for himself, and is determined and unyielding in its pursuit, he will not be thwarted by any adversity, and he will not give up until his dream come true. Here Confucius emphasizes the importance of setting an ambition for oneself. Having an ambition and coupling it with resolve and perseverance, you could make what seems impossible possible.

3. 子路、曾晳、冉有、公西华侍坐。子曰："以吾一日长乎尔，毋吾以也。居则曰：'不吾知也！'如或知尔，则何以哉？"子路率尔而对曰："千乘之国，摄乎大国之间，加之以师旅，因之以饥馑。由也为之，比及三年，可使有勇，且知方也。"夫子哂之。"求！尔何如？"对曰："方六七十，如五六十，求也为之，比及三年，可使足民。如其礼乐，以俟君子。""赤！尔何如？"对曰："非曰能之，愿学焉。宗庙之事，如会同，端章甫，愿为小相焉。""点！尔何如？"鼓瑟希，铿尔，舍瑟而作，对曰："异乎三子者之撰。"子曰："何伤乎？亦各言其志也。"曰："莫春者，春服既成，冠者五六人，童子六七人，浴乎沂，风乎舞雩，咏而归。"夫子喟然叹曰："吾与点也！"三子者出，曾晳后。曾晳曰："夫三子者之言何如？"子曰："亦各言其志也已矣。"曰："夫子何哂由也？"曰："为国以礼，其言不让，是故哂之。""唯求则非邦也与？""安见方六七十，如五六十，而非邦也者？""唯赤则非邦也与？""宗庙会同，非诸侯而何？赤也为之小，孰能为之大？"

五、理　想（Ideals）

今　译

　　子路、曾皙（曾点）、冉有（冉求）、公西华（公西赤）陪孔子坐着。孔子说："我是比你们年纪大一点，今天就不论年纪自由谈谈吧。你们平时总在说：'没有人知道我呀！'如果有人知道你们，那么你们打算怎么办呢？"子路不加思索地回答说："一个拥有一千辆兵车的国家，夹在大国之间，常受外国军队的侵犯，加上内部又有饥荒，如果让我去治理，等到三年的功夫，我就可以使人人勇敢善战，而且还懂得做人的道理。"孔子听了，微微一笑。孔子又问："冉求，你怎么样？"冉求回答说："一个纵横六七十里，或者五六十里的国家，如果让我去治理，等到三年，就可以使老百姓富足起来。至于修明礼乐，那就只得另请高明了。"孔子又问："公西赤，你怎么样？"公西赤回答说："我不敢说能够做到，只是愿意学习。在宗庙祭祀的事务中，或者在诸侯会盟，朝见天子时，我愿意穿着礼服，戴着礼帽，做一个小小的司礼。"孔子又问："曾点，你怎么样？"这时曾点弹瑟的声音逐渐稀疏了，接着铿的一声，放下瑟，直起身子回答说："我和他们三位的才能不一样呀！"孔子说："那有什么关系呢？不过是各自谈谈自己的志向罢了。"曾点说："暮春时节，春天的衣服已经穿上了。我和五六位成年人，六七个青少年，到沂河里洗洗澡，在舞雩台上吹吹风，一路唱着歌儿回来。"孔子长叹一声说："我是赞成曾点的想法呀！"子路、冉有、公西华三个人都出去了，曾皙留在后面。曾皙问："他们三位的话怎么样？"孔子说："也不过是各自谈谈自己的志向罢了。"曾皙说："您为什么笑仲由呢？"孔子说："治理国家要讲究礼让，可是他说话却一点也不谦让，所以我笑他。难道冉有所讲的就不是国家大事吗？哪里见得纵横六七十里或五六十里讲的就不是国家大事呢？公西赤所讲的不是国家大事吗？宗庙祭祀，诸侯会盟和朝见天子，讲的不是诸侯的大事又是什么呢？如果公西赤只能做个小小的司礼，那谁能去做大的司礼呢？"

Translation:

Zilu, Zeng Xi, Ran Qiu, and Gongxi Hua are in attendance by the Master. He says to them, "Let's disregard today that I'm older than you and engage in some unrestrained talk. You often lament, 'I am not known!' Now supposing someone were to recognize your merits, what employment would you choose?" Zilu hastily and elatedly replied, "Suppose a state of ten thousand chariots is sandwiched between two big powers and is repeatedly invaded and plagued by famines. Were I appointed to govern it, in three years of time I could make the people brave and moral." The Master smiles at him. Turning to Ranrou, he said, "Qiu, what are your wishes?" Ran You replies, "Entrust me with a state of sixty to seventy miles in length and give me a three-year grace, I will return an affluent society. As to teaching them the principles of etiquette and music, I must wait for the rise of a superior man to do that." "What are your wishes, Hua?" said the Master then to Gongxi Hua. Gongxi Hua replied, "I hesitate to claim that my ability is equal to these feats, but I wish to learn them. At the services of the ancestral temple, and at the audiences of the dukes with the Emperor, I should like, dressed in the ceremonial robe and the emblematic cap, to play the

五、理 想（Ideals）

acolyte master of ceremony." Last of all, the Master asks Zeng Xi, "Xi, what are your wishes?" Zeng Xi rose after softening his music on the lute and ending it with an accent note. "My ambition," he said, "is different from the cherished purposes of these three gentlemen." "It doesn't matter. It is only a revealing of personal wishes. So tell us your own." Zeng Xi then says, " Late spring, dressed for the season, in the company of five or six young men who have assumed the cap, and six or seven boys, I would bathe in River Yi, enjoy the breeze on the rain-altars, and return home singing." The Master heaves a sigh and says, "I give my approval to Zeng Xi." The three others having gone out, Zeng Xi remained behind, and says, "What do you think of the words of these three friends?" The Master replies, "They simply spoke out their wishes." Zeng Xi pursued, "Then why do you smile at Ran You?" The Master answers, "The management of a country demands comity. " His words are not modest. Therefore I smiled at him. Zeng Xi again asks, "Doesn't Ran You's aspiration have to do with the grand matters of a state?" The Master says, "Yes, did you ever see a territory of sixty or seventy miles, or one of fifty or sixty, which was not a state?" Once more, Zeng Xi requires, "Doesn't Gongxi Hua's aspiration have to do with the grand matters of a state?" The Master again replies, "Yes, who but princes have to do with ancestral temples, and audiences with the Emperor? If Gongxi Hua could only play the part of a junior assistant, who could play a major one?"

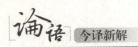

新 解

　　这是《论语》中最为有名的一段师生对话了，在这段对话中孔子以思想深沉的师长形象出现，他以平易近人的态度、诚恳发问的语气，启发四位学生各抒己见。从中我们也可以看出子路的率直、冉有、公西华的谦逊和曾晳的潇洒。子路志在治军，要在治军中展示他的才能；冉有志在从政，从为政中展示他的才能；公西华志在外交，从外交中展示他的才能。虽然他们一个比一个谦虚，但他们的理想都是"学为世用"，也就想要为国家做出力所能及的贡献。曾晳的志向则有所不同，要配合天时、地利、人和，由此自得其乐，随遇而安，展现了一种暮春三月，恬适潇洒的意境。这样的治平之世，居上位者无可为之事，处于社会下层的广大民众，人人安居乐业，无生老病死之虞。这种理想蓝图正是儒家的政治理想的体现，太平社会的缩影，孔子之所以欣赏曾晳的志向，显示了孔子在儒家深刻的入世情怀中，也有潇洒自在的意趣。

Contemporary interpretation:

　　This is the most known conversations among Confucius and his disciples. The conversation, with each participant's ambition as its topic, reveals Confucius' amiability and profundity. It also reveals Zilu's outspokenness, Ran You and Gongxi Hua's modesty and Zeng Xi's stoicism to fame and fortune. The three disciples' ambitions, respectively in the military, statecraft, and diplomacy, belong in nature to the same category though they are seemingly different. All concerns the disciples' wishes to serve the country. Only Zeng Xi is different.

五、理　想（Ideals）

His wish indicates a state of mind of pursuing personal freedom and social harmony. It could only be realized in a society in which the rulers have no trouble matters to tackle and the ordinary people live happily and have no worries about old pension and hospital expenses. This wish of Zeng Xi represents the political ideal of the Confucianists. It serves as a miniature of an affluent and peaceful society. Confucius's approval to Zing Xi's ambition also reveals his wishes of serving the country and living a happy, free, and idyllic life.

4. 子曰："志士仁人，无求生以害仁，有杀身以成仁。"

今　译

孔子说："有志者与行仁者，不会为了活命而背弃人生理想，却肯牺牲生命来成全人生理想。"

Translation:

The Master says, "The aspirant for nobility and virtue seeks not to preserve life by sacrificing his principles, but would rather, if need be, martyr his life for his principles."

新　解

"杀身成仁"是儒家道德的最高准则。这样的人不会为了生命的安全而放弃自己的追求和信仰。在建设新中国的革命战争中，千千万万的志士仁人为我们的革命事业抛头颅、洒热血，正是这一精神最崇高的体现。孟子后来的"舍生取义"，也是同样的意思，都是肯定人生应以实践道义为首要目标。这种思想影响深远，杀身成仁、舍生取义作为成语流传至今。

Contemporary interpretation:

"To die a martyr" is the supreme principle of Confucian morality. A person with such a principle will not barter his pursuit and belief for the safety of his life. This Confucianist belief could find its expression in the heroic deeds of those who had devoted their lives to the building of a new China during the Chinese civil war the Chinese Revolutions. Master Mencius' principle "Die for a just cause" expresses the same idea. Both principles advocate that as a human being we should put ideals and justice at the top priority of our concerns. This Confucian thought, having influenced hundreds of generations, has been bequeathed to us as a proverbial idiom.

5. 子曰："君子疾没世而名不称焉。"

今 译

孔子说："君子引以为憾的是：临到死时，没有好名声让

五、理 想 (Ideals)

人称述。"

Translation:

"A gentleman regrets a death that leaves no good reputation behind."

新 解

孔子认为一个仁人君子最大的遗憾是死了之后,在历史上无名无声,默默无闻。所以君子要把握有生之年努力奋斗。但是,在青史上留名,是要留好名声,而不是遗臭万年,留下好名是真正对历史有贡献。另外,一个真正的君子,都是严格要求自己,总是考量自己的学问、事业努力了多少,而不是简简单单地求出名。只要自己努力了,"桃李不言,下自成蹊",名声自然就传出去了。

Contemporary interpretation:

In Confucius' opinion, the greatest regret of a person with noble qualities and high ideas is that he has left no good reputation behind him and becomes oblivious. Therefore, a gentleman must make great efforts to accomplish a good name recorded in history. However, the Confucian teaching here is not an advocacy for single-minded pursuit of fame. A person—so long as he has done noble work—will have his good name spread far and near. Regarding recognition of our good deeds, learn from the peach and plum trees—they do not speak, yet a path is worn beneath them for their fruit-laden branches.

六、财　富（Wealth）

1. 子曰："富与贵，是人之所欲也；不以其道得之，不处也。贫与贱，是人之所恶也；不以其道得之，不去也。君子去仁，恶乎成名？君子无终食之间违仁，造次必于是，颠沛必于是。"

今　译

孔子说："富贵人人想要，如果不是正当方法得来的，宁可不要。贫贱人人讨厌，如果不是以正当方法脱离的，也宁可不脱离。君子如果与仁背道而驰，还算什么君子呢？就连一顿饭的工夫都不能违背仁，仓促匆忙时合乎仁，颠沛流离时也要合乎仁。"

Translation:

The Master says, "Riches and honors are what men desire, yet

六、财 富（Wealth）

should not be held if acquired wrongly. Poverty and obscurity are abhorred, yet should not be eliminated if the elimination is done wrongly. If a gentleman abandons virtue, then he is a gentleman no more. A gentleman does not, even for the space of a single meal, act contrary to virtue. In moments of haste, he cleaves to it. In seasons of danger, he cleaves to it as well."

新 解

这章说明仁是取舍一切的标准，是人须臾不可离弃的道德。孔子论述了具有仁心的人是怎样对待富贵贫贱的。富贵、功名与地位都是人所喜欢的，但是，不以正当途径得来，君子是不要的。贫与贱，是人人都讨厌的，即使一个有仁德修养的人，对贫贱也是不喜欢的，可是要用正当的方法致富，取得功名与地位，慢慢摆脱贫贱，而不是走歪门邪道。任何事业的成功都要依靠仁。君子在事业上取得成功，泰然处之；在失意时，也不颓丧、怨叹，不为环境所左右。顺利时要靠仁而成功，失意时要靠仁而安定。

Contemporary interpretation:

This analect teaches that virtue is the ultimate benchmark of a good life and is never to be abandoned. Here Confucius teaches people that wealth should be well-gotten instead of ill-gotten, and that poverty should be properly eliminated. When they are in good times, they should remain modest and composed, and when they are in bad times, they should refrain from being dejected and decadent. That is to say, they should not be completely influenced

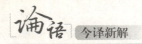

by the ever-changing environment.

---

2. 子曰："士志于道，而耻恶衣恶食者，未足与议也。"

今 译

孔子说："读书人立志追求人生理想，如果以简陋的衣服与粗糙的食物为可耻，那就不值得与他谈论什么人生道理了。"

Translation:

The Master says, "A scholar seeking the Way of Humanity yet ashamed of plain clothes and coarse food is not worthy to be counseled."

新 解

一个追求真理有远大理想的人，无暇顾及眼前的物质生活；同样，醉心于物质生活的人，很难是"有志于道"者。因为他的意志会被物质环境引诱、转移。一个只是贪图外在条件的人是无法和他谈学问、谈道理的。

Contemporary interpretation:

A person in pursuit of great ideals finds no time to fuss over material life. Similarly, a person indulgent in material hedonism hardly becomes one of great ideals. A person bent on materialistic ease will have his attention diverted astray and is thus not worthy of the discourse on scholarship and humanity.

3. 子曰:"放于利而行,多怨。"

今 译

孔子说:"做人处事全以利益来考量,就会招致许多怨恨。"

Translation:

The Master says, "A person, if solely motivated by self-profit, incites resentment."

新 解

一味追求个人的利益,一定会损害别人的利益,必然遭到被损害者的怨恨。就是一般的为人处事,也不能过分强调个人利益,以利为结合点,必然会因利害冲突而招致怨恨,例如交朋友若不是真诚以心相待,而是以利害相交,这种利害的结合,不会有好结果,最后还是以怨恨告终。

Contemporary interpretation:

If a person rivets his eyes only on his own interests, he

will impair those of others and surely will be grudged against. Therefore, in dealing with the others, we should not overemphasize our own interests and neglect that of others. Take making friends as an example. Friendship, for instance, if formed not out of mutual sincerity, but out of self-promotion, results in nothing but ill will.

4. 子曰："君子喻于义，小人喻于利。"

今 译

孔子说："君子行事考虑该不该做，小人行事考虑有没有好处。"

Translation:

The Master says, "A gentleman acts on the principle of social propriety; a snob, on personal gain."

新 解

人如果只有现实功利心而没有任何精神追求和价值信念，是令人鄙视的，是没有尊严可言的。当然，在现代商品经济社会中，个人和企业都要计算事业的损益和是否有利可图，因此不能简单化地去理解"利"。问题在于为人不能见利忘义，为追求利益不惜背信弃义，违背道德准则。孔子的核心思想就在

六、财　富（Wealth）

于此。

Contemporary interpretation:

A person driven by utilitarianism and mammonism is despicable and devoid of dignity. There is no denying that in modern society, the intercourses between people and between enterprises entail the consideration of each party's interests. And we should not simply label the interest-seeking activity as immoral. The essence of the Confucian teaching, however, is that pursuit of personal gain should never contravene moral principles.

5. 子曰："贤哉回也！一箪食，一瓢饮，在陋巷，人不堪其忧，回也不改其乐。贤哉回也！"

今　译

孔子说："颜回的德行真好啊！一竹盒饭，一瓢水，住在破旧的巷子里，别人都受不了这种苦，他却不改变自己原有的快乐。颜回的德行真好啊！"

Translation:

The Master says, "How admirable is Yan Hui, for he lives on a bowlful of rice, a gourd of water and in a small shabby lane. Others

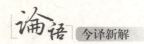

may find such austerity unbearable but Yan Hui delights in it. How admirable he is！"

新 解

本章孔子赞扬颜回安贫乐道的美德。颜回在人们不堪忍受的艰苦环境中致力于仁的追求,不减其乐,这实在是很难做到。物质环境如此恶劣,而心境竟然恬淡依旧,所以孔子用饱含深厚的感情赞叹颜回。后来,人们将这种不畏困苦而精进向上,一心求仁并以仁为乐的精神称为"孔颜乐处",即"孔子和颜回所乐之事"。

Contemporary interpretation:

In this statement Confucius praises Yan Hui's virtue of enjoying happiness amidst poverty. Coming from a poor family, Yan Hui was one of Confucius' favorite students. However, he was always in pursuit of humanity, taking delight in it and not distracted by his bad surroundings, and hence the expression "the delights of Confucius and Yan Hui's" which alludes to Confucius and Yan Hui's pursuit of true happiness.

6. 子曰:"富而可求也,虽执鞭之士,吾亦为之。如不可求,从吾所好。"

六、财 富（Wealth）

今 译

孔子说："财富如果可以求得，就算当个低贱的车夫，我也去做；如果无法以正当手段求得，那么还是追随我所爱好的理想吧。"

Translation:

The Master says, "If it gives wealth, even the menial work of a coachman I am willing to do. But if wealth is beyond my legitimate reach, I'd rather pursue my beloved ideals.

新 解

求富贵要靠自己的努力，只要是正当的职业，无所谓高低贵贱之分。可见孔子并不是不希望富贵，但如果用不合道义的手段去获得，那他宁可"安贫乐道"。

Contemporary interpretation:

Wealth should derive from legitimate efforts, which does not prejudice the prestigious professions over the obscure ones. What Confucius deprecates is not wealth, but ill-gotten wealth, and over the latter, he'd rather choose and delight in his ideals and be content in poverty.

7. 子曰:"饭疏食,饮水,曲肱而枕之,乐亦在其中矣。不义而富且贵,于我如浮云。"

今 译

孔子说:"吃的是粗食,喝的是冷水,弯起手臂做枕头,这样的生活也有乐趣啊!用不正当的手段得来的富贵,对我就好像浮云一样。"

Translation:

The Master says, "I can delight in eating coarse food, drinking cold water and pillowing on my elbow. To me, wealth obtained wrongly is phantasmal like drifting clouds."

新 解

孔子的这几句话,充分表达了他的人生观和价值观的核心。"富贵于我如浮云"更成为千百年来正直的知识分子的座右铭。富贵不是坏事,但如果用不合理的、非法的手段做到了又富又贵则是非常可耻的事。富贵就像天上的浮云一样聚散无常,稍纵即逝,不如仁义长久。人看穿了这一点,便不会受物质、环境、虚荣的诱惑,便会建立起自己的精神人格。一个人活着,只要具备最基本的生活条件,照样可以快乐。那些拥有巨大财富的人生活得未必快乐,而那些生活条件并不是很好的人,他们未必就不快乐。快乐是人内心的感受,并不是和物质条件成正比。

六、财 富（Wealth）

Contemporary interpretation:

This statement constitutes the kernel of Confucius' philosophy in life. His idea "Wealth obtained by illegitimate means is like a drifting cloud in the sky" has become a motto of the upright scholars and elites from generation to generation. Realization of the evanescence of wealth and the eternity of humanity will free a person from the corruption and temptation of mammonism. He could still take delight in an ordinary life so long as he is spiritually rich. Happiness is immanent and thus is neither dependent on nor proportionate to wealth, an external possession.

8. 子曰："贫而无怨难，富而无骄易。"

今 译

孔子说："贫穷而不抱怨，很难做到；富裕而不骄傲，则比较容易。"

Translation:

The Master says, "No complaint in poverty is a feat; no arrogance in wealth is a cinch."

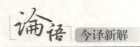

新 解

"贫"不一定指没有钱。贫穷、不得志、知识贫乏等等都是"贫"。人贫了就容易生怨,牢骚多,怨天尤人,所以孔子教人要做到"安贫乐道",但真正做到贫而能安,很不容易。孔子认为"富而无骄易",其实这个修养也很难。富贵了、地位高了、年纪大了都容易骄傲,容易看不起别人。

Contemporary interpretation:

Paucity, be it in money, success, or knowledge, incites complaints and grudges. Hence the Confucian teaching "Be contented in poverty and be delighted in the ideal," the accomplishment of which, however, is an admirable feat. Additionally, "humility in wealth" may not be a cinch, as thought by Confucius; wealth, status, and age in reality incline so many to be condescending.

七、孝 悌（Filial Piety and Fraternal Submission）

1. 有子曰："其为人也孝弟，而好犯上者，鲜矣；不好犯上，而好作乱者，未之有也。君子务本，本立而道生。孝弟也者，其为仁之本与！"

今 译

有子（有若）说："为人孝顺悌而爱好冒犯在上者的，很少见；不喜好冒犯在上者而喜好作乱的人，还从未有过。君子致力于根本，根本确立了，事物的基本道理就形成了。孝顺悌爱大概是实行仁的根本要点吧！"

Translation:

You Ruo says, "There are few who, being filial and fraternal, are fond of offending against their superiors. There have been none, who, not liking to offend against their superiors, have been fond of starting a riot. It is upon the upright trunk that the tree of the gentleman depends. That being established, the Way naturally grows up. Filial and fraternal submission! Are they not the trunk of virtue?"

新 解

这话虽是有子讲的，其所表达的无疑是孔子的思想。孝悌是孔子道德观的基础，是仁的根本。"仁"就是爱、爱别人。在当时宗法制度下，社会的政治结构建立在血宗关系基础上，对父兄孝悌也就是对天子国君忠顺，因而孝悌也就有了防止犯上作乱的作用。在孔子心目中这"仁"的根本在于亲情之爱，也就是要做到"仁"首先必须爱父母兄弟，否则谈"仁德"就是空话了！确实这样，如果一个人连和自己最亲近的父母兄弟都不爱，我们还有什么理由相信他会爱别人、爱国家呢？

Contemporary interpretation:

This statement, though made by You Ruo, reflects Confucian thought of filial piety and fraternal submission, both of which are the trunk of Confucian philosophy about virtue. Virtue, in Confucius' opinion, is to love. Under the feudal patriarchal clan system, the social structure was based on the clan ties. To be filial to one's father and respectful to one's elder brother is to be loyal to the monarch. Therefore, filial piety and fraternal submission may help prevent rebellions. In Confucian opinion, the essence of virtue is to love one's parents and respect one's brothers. If a person

七、孝 悌（Filial Piety and Fraternal Submission）

shows no love for his parents and no respect for his brothers, his talk of virtue and his love of others is questionable.

2. 子曰："弟子入则孝，出则悌，谨而信，泛爱众，而亲仁。行有余力，则以学文。"

今 译

孔子说："弟子在家要讲孝，在外要讲悌，言行要谨慎，要诚实可信，要广泛地爱众人，而亲近其中有仁德的人。这样做了还有余力和闲暇，再去学习文献知识。"

Translation:

The Master says, "A youth, when at home, should be filial, and when abroad, respectful to the elders. He should be circumspect and truthful. He should be loving to all and seek the company of the virtuous. If, when all these are performed and he still has energy to spare, let him study arts and literature."

新 解

这里提出孝悌、谨信、爱众、亲仁，是孔子对弟子们的基本要求，这些在今天也仍然是基本的道德要求。"孝悌"为"仁"之本，对人的爱首先应体现在对待亲人上，然后推及他人，这是"仁"的基本精神。其次，对父母、兄长恭孝，对朋友、他人讲信用，有爱心，这对规范当今社会关系有极其重要的关系。只有把这些基本的做人的基本准则学习好了，做到了，才能在此基础上学习知识。我们不能本末倒置，抛弃"根基"，一味强调"学"而忽视"修养"。

Contemporary interpretation:

In this statement Confucius put forth the basic principles a youth should follow if he is determined to cultivate his morality. The Confucian teaching that universal love starts with that for one's parents and respects for the elders is still applicable today in regulating social relations and building a harmonious society. A person, only after having cultivated and practiced all these principles of virtue, is eligible to study such polite arts as the *Book of Songs*, archery, and deportment. Knowledge acquisition, if put above moral edification, is like the cart put before the horse.

3. 子曰："父在，观其志；父没，观其行；三年无改于父之道，可谓孝矣。"

今 译

孔子说："父亲在世，观察他的志向；父亲去世，观察他

七、孝 悌（Filial Piety and Fraternal Submission）

的行为。三年不改变父亲的准则，可以说是孝了。"

Translation:

The Master says, "A youth could be judged by his ambition when his father is alive and by his conducts when his father is alive no more. If he could adhere to his father's way of managing the home for three years, he could be said to be a filial son."

新 解

"孝"是子女对父母的感激之情和爱。古希腊伦理学大师亚里士多德说："我们应当帮助父母大于帮助其他任何人，因为我们对父母欠有养育之恩，我们还应该对父母表示敬意，正如对神表示敬意一样。"儒家认为，孝包括赡养父母，但主要不在于生活方面，而在于感情上的抚慰。父母最感欣慰的莫过于子女有所作为，因此，"三年无改于父道"就是为了回报父母之爱，遵循父亲的训诫也是孝的一种具体表现。现代社会在发展，人们的思想观念也应追随社会的发展而适时地做出调整，这也是历史发展的必然。我们要孝顺，也不能愚孝，不能一味地顺从父母的陈旧规则。当然其中合理的部分可以予以保留。

Contemporary interpretation:

Filial piety reflects a person's gratitude and love for his parents. The ancient Greek moralist Aristotle said, "We should help our parents more than do anyone else as we owe them the debt of raising us. We should revere our parents the same way as do our God". Confucianism thinks that filial piety may find its expression in feeding and clothing one's parents when they are advanced in years, but the better part of its essence is to be attached to one's parents emotionally and offer timely comforts whenever the need is be. In a certain way, the utmost comfort a filial person could offer to his parents is to become established in the competitive society. The father finds no greater pride than in a successful son. And adherence to the word and example of one's father no doubt is part of filial piety. However, changes and developments in society entail moral adaptations. Filial piety, though a virtue in itself, should not be practiced as blind submission to the parents, whose outmoded and inappropriate requirements may also call for a reaction of revision and reservation.

---

4. 子游问孝。子曰:"今之孝者,是谓能养。至于犬马,皆能有养。不敬,何以别乎?"

今 译

子游询问孝,孔子说:"现今的孝是指能养活。人们对狗马都能饲养,如果只知供给父母衣食而不示恭敬,这与饲养动物有什么区别呢?"

Translation:

Ziyou counsels the Master on filial piety. The Master says,

七、孝 悌（Filial Piety and Fraternal Submission）

"Nowadays what people mean by filial piety is merely providing for one's parents, but dogs and horses are also provided for. So without paying respect for one's parents, how is the distinction to be made?"

新 解

这章强调了真正的"孝"是以恭敬为本的。孝不单单是去用物质来充实父母的生活，不能只是说我尽到养的责任了，还要有发自内心的敬重。如果没有敬重，养父母和养狗，就没有区别了。

Contemporary interpretation:

This statement accentuates reverence as the essence of filial piety. To Confucius, filial piety entails not only care of, but more importantly, heart-felt respect for the parents. Filling parents' pockets with money and surrounding them with material things do not mean that one has fulfilled his filial duty. The material things, only when coupled with emotional attachment and frequent visits, could mean something to one's parents. Without reverence to the parents, mere care of the parents' physical and material life cannot be distinguished from the care of dogs.

---

5. 季康子问："使民敬、忠以劝，如之何？"子曰："临之以庄，则敬；孝慈，则忠；举善而教不能，则劝。"

论语 今译新解

今 译

季康子问:"要令百姓尊敬,忠诚而又勤劳,怎样才能做到呢?"孔子说:"用庄重的心态面对大家,他们就会尊敬你。领导者具备尊老爱幼的高尚品德,百姓就会忠心于你。表扬有能力的人、树立榜样来教导百姓,他们就会勤奋努力。"

Translation:

Ji Kang asks the Master, "How to instill in the people the values of respect, loyalty, and industry?" The Master replies, "They will revere you when you approach them with solemnity. They will pledge you allegiance if you respect the elderly and care for the young. They will emulate the competent that is lauded as the exemplary."

新 解

从家庭来说,子女对父母要孝,父母对子女要慈。从国家来说,为政者对父母要孝,对人民要慈,这样人民才能信服自己。庄、孝慈、(举)善,都是个人的品德和修为,同时也是政治人物非常重要的"德能"。孔子在这里强调的是一种以上化下的表率作用,通过自身的美德来感化、教育、管理百姓,而不是用权术来欺骗,这便是孔子"以德治国"的核心思想。

Contemporary interpretation:

In a harmonious family, children should be filial to their

七、孝 悌 (Filial Piety and Fraternal Submission)

parents and parents kind to their children. In a harmonious nation, the governor should be filial to his parents and kind to his people. This is the prerequisite for receiving trust from the people. Effective statecraft implicates the practice of solemnity, filial duty, clemency, and kindness. What Confucius emphasizes here is the modeling function of the superiors. "Government by virtue," a central teaching by Confucius, means that a good statesman influences through example, not manipulates through crafty deception.

6. 子曰："事父母几谏，见志不从，又敬不违，劳而不怨。"

今 译

孔子说："服侍父母时，发现父母有什么过错，要委婉劝阻；看到自己的心意没有被接受，仍然要恭敬地不触犯他们，内心忧愁但是不去抱怨。"

Translation:

The Master says, "In serving our parents, if we find some fault in them, we should advise them gently. If they do not take any heed, we should still respect them rather than offend them. While we worry about them, we should not blame them."

新 解

在家里,做子女的必须要孝敬父母,这是中国社会的传统美德。但是父母也是人,自然可能说错话、办错事,遇到这种情况,子女要注意劝谏的方法:用和善的态度对待,事先就委婉相劝,使父母认识错误直至改正,千万不能粗言恶语。如果行不通,仍要保持恭敬、孝敬父母的心态。因为就算父母犯了很大的错,始终是我们的父母,子女内心始终应祝福、祈祷父母能回头,不要存怨恨之心。

Contemporary interpretation:

Being filial to one's parents is a traditional virtue of the Chinese people. Just as what is put in the saying "To err is human," so it is quite natural that our parents will make some mistakes in daily life. When such cases arise, young people should not point out their parents' mistakes bluntly and offensively. Gentle innuendos may be employed to approach these mistakes. In these cases, vitriolic words are not to be considered. Even when our gentle innuendos fall upon deaf ears, the parents are still to be respected, as even a grave blunder by our parents cannot change the very fact that they are our parents, whom we should forever hold in our blessing and prayer, and never in our resentment.

七、孝 悌（Filial Piety and Fraternal Submission）

7. 子曰："父母在，不远游，游必有方。"

今 译

孔子说："父母在世的时候，不要出远门。如果非去不可的话，也要明确告知父母自己所要去的地方。"

Translation:

The Master says, "No travel far afield when parents are alive. Parents must know your itinerary if you have to travel."

新 解

古时候交通不发达，行程很慢，出门动辄三五个月，甚至是三五年，而且通讯也不容易，很容易失去联系。儿行千里母担忧，所以子女出门让父母非常操心。但现代社会大不相同了，交通、通讯非常发达，外出时安顿好父母，经常与家人沟通联系。能够让家人知道平安，父母对出门的子女也不会像古人那样牵肠挂肚了，只要能够做到有时间常回家看看就行了。

Contemporary interpretation:

In ancient times, neither transportation nor communication was convenient. A long journey often meant an absence of months and even years. In such circumstances, it was very easy for the traveler to lose contact with his family, hence the Chinese saying,

"A son in sojourn means a mother in solicitude." Now times have changed and both transportation and communication have become very convenient. Young people should ease their qualms about working far from home. So long as they keep their communication with and their visits to their parents frequent, their parents will not suffer the kind of anxiety as the ancient parents did.

8. 子曰:"父母之年,不可不知也。一则以喜,一则以惧。"

今 译

孔子说:"父母的年龄是不可以不知道的。人们一方面因父母高寿而高兴,一方面因父母的衰老而恐惧。"

Translation:

The Master says, "Know the age of parents so as to show our joy to their longevity and our solicitude to their senility."

新 解

孔子说:做子女的人对父母的年龄不能不知道。但是又会产生两种心理,一方面因为知道父母的年龄多了一岁,为他们增寿而高兴;但同时又害怕,因为父母年岁越高,距离人生的

七、孝 悌（Filial Piety and Fraternal Submission）

终点越近，做儿女的能与父母相处行孝的时间就越短。孔子这句话的目的是教育人们应看到父母年寿日高而及时行孝，以成孝道。

Contemporary interpretation:

It is a lucky thing that our parents could live a long life. An advanced age of our parents is always a matter of ambivalence, signifying both longevity and senescence. The purpose of Confucius' remark is to prompt young people to practice filial piety to their parents while they are still healthy and alive. Filial piety should be perceived and enjoyed by our parents rather than seen and praised by the outsiders.

9. 宰我问："三年之丧，期已久矣。君子三年不为礼，礼必坏；三年不为乐，乐必崩。旧谷既没，新谷既升，钻燧改火，期可已矣。"子曰："食夫稻，衣夫锦，于女安乎？"曰："安！""女安则为之。夫君子之居丧，食旨不甘，闻乐不乐，居处不安，故不为也。今女安，则为之。"宰我出。子曰："予之不仁也！子生三年，然后免于父母之怀。夫三年之丧，天下之通丧也。予也有三年之爱于其父母乎？"

今译

宰我请教说:"为父母守丧三年,时间未免太长了。君子三年不举行礼仪,礼仪一定会荒废;三年不演奏音乐,音乐一定会散乱。旧谷吃完,新谷也已收成;打火的燧木轮用了一次。所以守丧一年就可以了。"孔子说:"守丧未满三年,就吃白米饭,穿锦缎衣,你心里安不安呢?"宰我说:"安。"孔子说:"你心安,就去做吧!君子在守丧时,吃美食不辨滋味,听音乐不感快乐,住家里不觉舒适,所以不这么做。现在你既然心安,就去做吧!"宰我退出房间后,孔子说:"宰我没有真诚的情感啊!一个孩子生下来,三年以后才能离开父母的怀抱。为父母守丧三年,天下人都是这么做的。宰我难道就不能守孝三年回报父母的恩爱吗?"

Translation:

Zaiwo says to the Master, "Mourning for three years is too long. If a gentleman does not follow rituals for three years, he will be out of practice. If he does not play on his musical instrument for three years, his music will fall into disarray. When the old grains have been eaten, new grains will arrive. The kindling flint has been used for a full cycle. Therefore, mourning for one year is long enough." The Master asks, "Do you feel comfortable eating new grains and wearing new clothes only one year after your father's decease?" Zaiwo answers, "I do." "If you feel comfortable, then go ahead and do it. During the mourning period, a gentleman has no taste for fine food, nor has he taste for happy music, nor does

七、孝 悌 (Filial Piety and Fraternal Submission)

he feel at ease living at home. That is why he does not eat new grains nor wear new clothes. Since you do not scruple against these precepts, you can go ahead and do it." When Zaiwo is gone, the Master says, "Zaiwo has no true love for his parents. Children practically spend their first three years of life in the arms of their parents, so this practice of mourning for three years is universally accepted. Why Zaiwo alone could not perform the ritual of mourning for three years to repay his parents' deep love?"

新 解

在古代，丧礼是非常重视的，在现代社会的要求则不一样。孔子是比较保守的，他极力主张维持孝道，主张依照古礼。孔子认为小孩子三岁才能离开父母的怀抱，后来二十年的养育且不去管，这三年的感情如何去还。所以服丧三年，就是对于父母怀抱了我们三年，把我们抚养长大了的一点点还报，这是适应情感需要而制定的。如果没有这份真诚的感情，在丧期中照样吃喝玩乐也可以心安理得，那么三年之丧就失去了意义。所以，这里的礼不是表面的形式，而是人内心情感的反映。归根结底，孔子是教人对父母付出的爱心心存感恩，关键在"心安"，而不在守丧年期的长短，否则"孝"只是一句空话、一套形式。我们现在由于种种原因，不可能拘泥于旧时的守孝之礼，但对于饱含在守孝之中的情意应当领会，常怀孝悌仁爱之心，并将此推广开去，使这些行为规范成为发自内心的自觉的要求。

Contemporary interpretation:

The modern society, different from ancient times, accords much

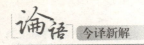

less importance to mourning ceremony. Confucius, a conservative saint, thinks that people should observe the ancient mourning ceremony to the letter. According to his point of view, mourning over one's parent's death for three years is the child's repayment of the parent's lavish care and love in the child's first three years. If a person feels no sincere sorrow for his parent's decease and still eats and drinks extravagantly during his parent's mourning period, the practice of the mourning ceremony becomes meaningless. Therefore, the ceremony should not become a mere formality, but should be a medium through which the living is able to express their sincere sorrow and lament. In essence, what Confucius intends to convey to the young is that they should be grateful to their parents for what they have done to them and feel true sorrow for their passing away. As for the mourning ceremony, what matters is the true feelings instead of the duration of the mourning period. Today, on account of various reasons we could not perform the mourning ceremony the same way as Confucius advocates, but we should understand the essence embodied in the process and have it realized whenever we are put in such a situation.

> 10. 子夏问孝。子曰："色难。有事，弟子服其劳；有酒食，先生馔，曾是以为孝乎？"

七、孝 悌（Filial Piety and Fraternal Submission）

今 译

子夏请教什么是孝。孔子说："子女保持和悦的脸色是最难的。有事要办时，让年轻人代劳；有酒菜食物时，让年长的人先吃喝；这样就可以算是孝了吗？"

Translation:

Zixia asks the Master about filial piety. The Master says, "To wear a pleasing and gracious face before one's parents is most difficult. Doing things for them and leaving the best food to them are filial actions. But is it what filial piety truly mean?"

新 解

孝敬父母不只是替父母做事或者把好酒好菜让父母先吃。如果说出来的话、表现出来的神情让人难以接受，即使替父母把事情做了，好饭菜让他们吃了，也不算真正的孝。孝顺出于子女爱父母之心，这种爱心自然表现为和悦的神情与温和的脸色。心敬是内，态度和悦是外。看来，态度和悦的确比为父母做事或请父母吃饭要困难多了。在现代社会的家庭中，孝敬父母仍然是家庭和谐的必不可少的因素。

Contemporary interpretation:

Practicing filial piety does not only mean providing for and doing things for the parents' comfort. It also means wearing a meek and amicable face before them. Yet to the parents, if the word is harsh and the countenance is a frown, no filial piety is possible. Filial piety, though an inner state of respect and love in the heart, finds its outward expression in the child's clement words and pleasing face. All this may prove more difficult than the mere action of attending and feeding the parents. Even for a harmonious family in modern times, genuine filial piety is indispensable.

八、交 友（Making Friends）

1. 子贡问友。子曰："忠告而善道之，不可则止，毋自辱焉。"

今 译

子贡请教交友之道。孔子说："朋友若有过错，要真诚相告而委婉劝导；他若不肯听从，就闭口不说，以免自取其辱。"

Translation:

Zigong asks about friendship. The Master says, "If you see faults in your friends, frankly admonish them and tactfully guide them. If they do not listen, let them be. Do not disgrace yourself."

新 解

本章是孔子讲交朋友的方法，即"忠告而善道之。"孔子认为对待朋友要尽我们的忠心，劝勉他，好好诱导他，实在没有办法的时候，也犯不着苛求于人，适可而止。假如过分了，反而自讨没趣。朋友是要"规过劝善"，有错误相互纠正，彼此向好的方向勉励，这是真朋友，但是规过劝善也有一定的限度。与人相处要恰到好处，这是孔子从生活实践中积累起来的处世哲学。

Contemporary interpretation:

In this chapter Confucius teaches about friendship. The master thinks that we should be frank in pointing out the faults and shortcomings of our friends. If the friend refuses to listen, we should not force him to accept our advice for this will probably incur disgrace for ourselves. There is no denying that true friends should be open-minded to each other and admonish each other. But we must carry out the admonishing obligation to a proper degree. Admonition, if overdone, will incur our friends' resentment.

2. 曾子曰："君子以文会友，以友辅仁。"

今　译

曾子说："君子用文章来聚会朋友，用朋友来帮助自己培养仁德。"

八、交　友 (Making Friends)

Translation:

Master Zeng says, "A gentleman on literary grounds meets with his friends, and by their friendship perfects his virtue."

新　解

曾子所说的交友之道，是结交志同道合的朋友，以文会友，切磋琢磨于义理之会，互相促进，这样既提高了学术水平，又提高自己的道德修养，这才是正确的交友原则。

Contemporary interpretation:

Master Zeng advocates befriending those that share your aspirations. Real friends should promote each other's scholarly and moral pursuits to bring about the realization of their own literary talents and moral edification.

---

3. 子曰："不得中行而与之，必也狂狷乎。狂者进取，狷者有所不为也。"

今　译

孔子说："找不到言行合乎中庸的人来往，就一定要找到狂放的人和狷介的人。狂放的人奋发上进，狷介的人能洁身自好。"

Translation:

The Master says, "If one cannot find and interact with practitioners of the Doctrine of the Mean well he will have to befriend the ardent and the discreet. The former are enterprising and the latter will keep them from what is wrong."

新解

孔子认为如果一时找不到合乎中道的人谈论道德学问，则宁可退而求其次和进取心强或谨守气节而有所不为的人相交。这也启发我们，交朋友不能过于苛求，完美无缺的人在世上能有多少呢？看人主要看本质，如果本质不错，不是浑浑噩噩，即使有这样那样的缺点还是可以帮助他改进的。

Contemporary interpretation:

In Confucius' opinion, if we cannot find those who are perfect to communicate with, we might as well befriend those who are ambitious or overcautious, for both types of people have something desirable for us to learn from. This statement of Confucius teaches us that in making friends we should not become exacting perfectionists. A person, so long as he is not wicked in nature, must have something good in him. Such a person, though not an ideal model for us, is worthy of our friendship. We could even help him revise his mistakes by means of our friendship.

八、交 友（Making Friends）

4. 子曰："群居终日，言不及义，好行小慧，难矣哉！"

今 译

孔子说："一群人整天相处在一起，说的是无关道义的话，又喜欢卖弄小聪明，实在很难走上人生正途！"

Translation:

The Master says, "The virtuous way may be impervious to those who spend their day, not discoursing on humanity, but flaunting their petty smartness."

新 解

交友要交益友，对自己有帮助的朋友。如果交些不思上进的朋友，大家在一起，讲起话来没有什么内容，也无正事可谈，整日虚度光阴，做事浮夸，人慢慢就堕落了。

Contemporary interpretation:

Befriend those salubrious to you. Interaction with those that lack enterprise promotes nothing but vacuity, idleness, ostentation, and even depravity.

5. 孔子曰："益者三友，损者三友。友直，友谅，友多闻，益矣。友便辟，友善柔，友便佞，损矣。"

今 译

孔子说："三种朋友有益，三种朋友有害。与正直的人为友，与诚信的人为友，与见多识广的人为友，那是有益的；与装腔作势的人为友，与刻意讨好的人为友，与巧言善辩的人为友，那是有害的。"

Translation:

The Master says, "There are three types of salubrious friends and three types of detrimental ones. Friends who are upright, sincere and experienced are salubrious. Friends who are pretentious, ingratiating, and grandiloquent are detrimental."

新 解

在现代社会中交朋友的机会很多，重要的是在交往过程中，怎样加深认。孔子告诉了我们识别的标准：讲直话、个性宽厚、知识渊博的人。孔子把这三种人列为对个人有益的朋友。而那些有怪癖的人、巧言善辩的人、专门逢迎拍马的人都是朋友中有害的。真正的贤友固然多多益善，不过就算只有两三个，也就够一辈子得益了。交友不当，后果有时不堪设想。由此可见，交友不可不慎，宁缺毋滥。

八、交 友 (Making Friends)

Contemporary interpretation:

There are many opportunities to make friends. Here Confucius provides us with the touchstone to test beneficial friendship. In his opinion, we should make friends with those who are frank, kind-hearted and learned, for they are beneficial to us. And we should shun those who are eccentric, snobbish, glib-tongued and ingratiating, for they are harmful to us. Real good friends, though numbered few, will bring about benefits to us all our life. However, a bad friend will bring about unimaginable harm to us. Friendship should be a cautious business; better fewer if good than more if bad.

九、处 世（Conducting Oneself in Society）

1. 子曰："君子不重，则不威。学则不固。主忠信。无友不知己者。过则勿惮改。"

今 译

孔子说："君子不庄重就会没有威严，多方学习就不会流于固执。以忠信为人处事的原则，不与那些不忠信的人交往。有了过错，不要避讳，要去积极改正。"

Translation:

The Master says, "If solemn, a gentleman will be august. If learned, a scholar will be magnanimous. Practice fidelity and shun those unequal to your virtue. Own your mistakes and rectify them."

九、处　世（Conducting Oneself in Society）

新　解

孔子强调君子要庄重，实际上是让人保持自尊心，自重则他重，如果自己都不自重，谁还能信任你呢？"无友不知己者"，是说不要与那些道德修养低的人，并非泛指一般的不如己者，因为近朱者赤、近墨者黑，长期耳濡目染那些下流的东西也会影响到自己的道德修养。人非圣贤，孰能无过？过错一经发现，就要勇于改过，才是真学问、真道德。

Contemporary interpretation:

Confucius here teaches the importance of dignified demeanor, which begets respect. "Shun those unequal to you" means exclusion of people morally lower than you. This, however, should not be applied to those who are economically or intellectually inferior to you. Confucius's opinion actually corresponds with the Chinese saying, "A person, when close to crimson, he will be stained with it and becomes crimson; when close to ink, he will be stained with it and becomes inky." To err is human. The crux of the matter lies in that a gentleman must be truly learned and moral. Whenever he makes a mistake, he will lose no time to correct it.

2. 子贡问君子。子曰："先行其言，而后从之。"

今 译

子贡问什么是君子。孔子说:"事事做在先,说在后,这样的人才是君子"

Translation:

Zigong asks the Master about being a gentleman. The Master says, "A gentleman always acts before he talks."

新 解

本章讲的是做事要少说空话,多做实事,言行一致。俗话说"一言九鼎"、"一诺千金",孔子对君子的要求则更高,不仅仅是"说了就做",而是"做了再说"。孔子一贯主张言行一致,作为君子凡事要把实际行动摆在前面,不要总说大话,实际上却做不到,这样肯定会被人看扁。而是应该先做,起表率作用,做完了,大家看在眼里,自然会听从你、敬佩你。也就是说,不要做嘴的巨人,行动的矮子。真正的君子笃言慎行,他们不自负地标榜自己,却用行动告诉你他们的修养品性。可见孔子主张言行一致,反对言行不一,而且重在用、重在行。

Contemporary interpretation:

This statement teaches us that in real life we should do much and talk little, and that our deeds must agree with our words. Beyond the Chinese saying, "A promise weighs as the mountain

九、处 世 (Conducting Oneself in Society)

and is valued the same as a thousand tales of gold," the Confucian precept for the gentleman is more rigorous: act before speech. In other words, we should avoid becoming a giant in speech but a dwarf in action. A true gentleman is cautious in speech and serious in action. He never pretentiously flaunts himself. So long as he lets out a word, he will overcome all difficulties to fulfill it. From this statement we can see that Confucius puts emphasis on the congruence between our words and our deeds. To him, what counts is a person's actions instead of his words.

3. 子曰:"君子怀德,小人怀土;君子怀刑,小人怀惠。"

今 译

孔子说:"君子考虑的是道德,小人考虑的是土地;君子考虑的是法度,小人考虑的是恩惠。"

Translation:

The Master says, "The gentleman prizes virtue; the vulgarian, land. The gentleman worries about lawful punishment; the vulgarian, personal gain."

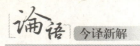

新 解

这里对比了君子与小人两者之间不同的人生观和价值观：君子念念不忘的是道德修养和怕做错事受法律制裁，违反道德的事不做。而小人只关心利益，不管道德与否，只要有利益就行。这正是判断谁是君子、谁是小人的标准。

Contemporary interpretation:

Here Confucius makes a vivid contrast between different outlooks of life and concepts of values held respectively by the gentleman and the ignoble person. What a gentleman is obsessed with is moral lifting and punishment receiving, whereas what an ignoble person is obsessed with is benefits seeking and law loophole studying. Confucius' clear dichotomy between the two types of person could help us to see clear who is who.

---

4. 子曰："不患无位，患所以立；不患莫己知，求为可知也。"

今 译

孔子说："不担心没有官位，要担心的是凭什么立身处世。不担心没有人了解自己，要设法使自己值得让别人了解。"

九、处 世（Conducting Oneself in Society）

Translation:

The Master says, "Worry not whether there is an office for me, but what enables me to befit the office. Worry not that nobody knows me, but whether my doing is worthy of knowing."

新 解

人活世上，人人都想谋得理想的职位，最怕的是自己没有真本领站得起来。"酒香不怕巷子深"，不怕没有人了解自己，只要有真才实学，有真本领，干出事情，别人自然能知道你，这样就不愁谋不到好职位，不愁没有施展才能的机会。本章中孔子勉励学生严格要求自己，掌握真正的坚实的立世本领。

Contemporary interpretation:

It is understandable that every person wants to acquire a favorable social position. From this statement, we can see that even Confucius do not deny this point. Yet cultivation of the capabilities required by the position must precede acquisition of the position. Just as described in the Chinese saying, "The wine, if fragrant, sells even hidden deep in the lane," a capable person needs not worry about temporary obscurity. Here Confucius encourages his students to get prepared in advance for a better chance.

5. 子曰："古者言之不出，耻躬之不逮也。"

今 译

孔子说:"古时候的人不轻易把话说出口,就怕自己的行为跟不上而引以为耻。"

Translation:

The Master says, "The ancients were wary with their own words for they were afraid of bearing the shame of not being able to keep their word."

新 解

孔子认为古代的人不肯乱讲话,就是怕自己的行为做不到。言行一致是做人的道德准则,说话和行动必须一致,怎么说就怎么做,说到就要做到。有信义的人往往不轻易允诺,一旦说出口,历经千难万险也会努力去兑现,所谓"轻死生,重然诺"。

Contemporary interpretation:

Here Confucius, by alluding to the ancient people, maintains that the supreme principle a person should follow is that his words must correspond with his deeds. A person with credit should make a promise very cautiously. Once he makes it, he must manage to keep it under whatever difficulties. This is just what is meant by valuing one's promise more than one's life.

九、处 世（Conducting Oneself in Society）

6. 子曰："奢则不孙，俭则固。与其不孙也，宁固。"

今 译

孔子说："奢侈就显得骄纵，节俭就显得寒碜。与其选择骄纵，宁可选择寒碜。"

Translation:

The Master says, "Extravagance leads easily to presumption, and frugality easily to dowdiness. But dowdiness is still superior to presumption."

新 解

在孔子看来，奢与俭都有缺陷，奢往往会骄纵僭上，俭往往会固陋吝啬。过与不及，两者都不符合中庸之道，不合于礼，最好是既不奢侈，也不俭约，恰到好处。在不能做到这一点时，权衡两者，孔子主张宁俭而弗奢。

Contemporary interpretation:

In Confucius' opinion, neither extravagance nor frugality is flawless. Extravagance usually leads to insubordination, and frugality usually worsens into penuriousness. Neither is in keeping with the Doctrine of Mean. And neither follows the protocol of decorum. The ideal is freedom from both. If this proves impossible, choose frugality over extravagance.

7. 子曰："君子坦荡荡，小人长戚戚。"

今 译

孔子说："君子心里坦坦荡荡，小人心里充满忧愁。"

Translation:

The Master says, "A gentleman's heart is wide-open; an ignoble person's, worry-laden."

新 解

君子不怨天尤人，胸襟开朗，以舒畅平和的心态看待世间的美好与丑恶，内心便是平静和安详的。小人胸襟狭小，容不下任何人，他们没有真正的朋友，整天在心里算计小利，患得患失，他的痛苦和烦恼也是一生没有穷尽。放下成见，快乐便会油然而生。这两句可以作为座右铭，时刻提醒自己。

Contemporary interpretation:

A gentleman is always open-minded and he could look at world affairs with a calm heart, never complaining about others.

九、处 世 (Conducting Oneself in Society)

Such a person could enjoy inner peace and composure all his life. Whereas an ignoble person is always narrow-minded and could not swallow the slightest offence by others, concerned always about personal gains and losses. Such a person will suffer from worries and vexations all his life. Live by the motto of this Confucian teaching and your heart will be free from offensive prejudice and replete with serene joy.

8. 子曰:"笃信好学,守死善道。危邦不入,乱邦不居。天下有道则见,无道则隐。邦有道,贫且贱焉,耻也;邦无道,富且贵焉,耻也。"

今 译

孔子说:"坚定地相信大道,努力学习它,誓死保全它。不进入危亡的国家,不居留在祸乱的国家。天下有道就出来从政,天下无道就隐退不出。国家有道,自己贫穷低贱,是耻辱;国家无道,富有尊贵,是耻辱。"

Translation:

The Master says, "Learn and espouse the Way with your life. Do not join a state in disintegration. Do not reside in a state in agitation. Practice statesmanship when the Way prevails in the state. Live in solitude when the Way is absent in the state. Shameful is a life of abject poverty in a well-governed state. Shameful is a life of extravagant wealth in an ill-governed state."

新　解

在一个贪污腐败、卖官买官、投机倒把的国家，如果你既有钱又有地位，那你一定也是用不正当的手段得来的。在一个法律严明、政府廉洁、自由民主的国家，你却非常贫穷，那一定是你不够努力。实行正道，也要看时机。儒家讲"穷则独善其身，达则兼济天下"，不论哪种处境都要做到安之泰然。

Contemporary interpretation:

If you are moneyed and honored in a corrupt and lawless state, you have no right to flaunt your social position because what you possess must have been got by ill means. If you are poor and lowly in a prosperous and lawful state, you have no right to complain about your conditions because your predicament must be the result of your indolence. Virtue has its own time and needs to be practiced in accordance with genuine humanity. "When a person is down and out he is supposed to take good care of himself and when he is prosperous he is supposed to serve the society." Under either condition, we must live in serene repose.

九、处　世（Conducting Oneself in Society）

9. 子曰："不在其位，不谋其政。"

今　译

孔子说："不在那个职位上，不要去考虑那个职位的政务。"

Translation:

The Master says, "If not appointed into the position, meddle not with its obligation."

新　解

孔子这样说主要是想让每个人都立足于做好自己的本职工作。不要自己的工作没有做好，却对别人的工作指手画脚，说三道四，于事于己都没有好处。从积极方面说，"不在其位，不谋其政"，可以防止越权处理问题，干预他人正常地进行职权范围内的工作。很多人拿孔子的这句话当挡箭牌，耍滑头，推托事情，这就不对了。公民有监督政府的权利，新闻媒体有批评政府错误的权利，学者、智囊有为政府出谋划策的职责，这就要"不在其位，也谋其政"。

Contemporary interpretation:

What Confucius implies here is that as a social member each person should do his own business well and avoid finding faults with others before proper completion of their own obligations. Positively, this Confucian teaching reminds us avoiding overstepping our privileges and meddling into others' province of administration. Negatively, some play smart with this Confucian teaching and use it as pretext for shirking their responsibilities and camouflaging their malfeasance. In modern society, each person has the right to supervise the running of the government and each form of medium has the right to criticize the mistakes of the government. Everybody, not only scholars and those think tanks, has the duty to give suggestions to the government. That is to say, even we are not in the position, we should concern ourselves with the work for it.

10. 司马牛忧曰："人皆有兄弟，我独亡！"子夏曰："商闻之矣，死生有命，富贵在天。君子敬而无失，与人恭而有礼。四海之内皆兄弟也，君子何患乎无兄弟也？"

今 译

司马牛忧愁地说："人们都有兄弟，唯独我没有。"子夏说："我听说，人的死生由命主宰，富贵由天安排，君子只要敬业不犯错误，对人恭敬有礼，天下的人都是自己的兄弟。君子又何必担忧没有兄弟呢？"

Translation:

Sima Niu says sadly, "Other people have brothers and I alone

九、处　世（Conducting Oneself in Society）

have none." Zixia says, "I have heard that a person's life and death are a matter of destiny, and that his poverty and richness are at the disposal of Heaven. A gentleman, if conscientious in his work and polite to the others, could enjoy brotherhood wherever he goes. So why do you worry that you have no brothers?"

新　解

司马牛有很多的兄弟，向魋、向巢、子欣、子车都是他的兄弟，他们在宋国专权，且又将发动叛乱。因而司马牛感到凄然孤立而有无兄弟之忧。其实，司马牛也是担忧向魋等叛乱而遭灭族，自己将受到株连。所以子夏劝子牛要认识到一切都是命中注定，看开一些，不要自我封闭。只要待人诚恳，以天下人为兄弟，那么到处都有你的兄弟。"四海之内皆兄弟也"也成为千古名言。

Contemporary interpretation:

Sima Niu actually had several brothers. Xiang Kui, Xiang Chao, Zixin and Ziche were all his blood brothers. They all held high positions in the state Song and were plotting a revolt. Their plot was finally discovered and they were severely punished with the sentence of death or exile. So Sima Niu felt alone after the incident. In a sense, Sima Niu was worrying that he might become incriminated and get punished. Therefore, Zixia is comforting him by saying that everything is predestined, that he should bravely face the reality as it was, and that so long as he himself is polite and virtuous he will have brothers within the Four Seas, hence the ancient Chinese apothegm

"All men are brothers within the Four Seas."

---

11. 子曰:"君子成人之美,不成人之恶。小人反是。"

今 译

孔子说:"君子成全人家的好事,不促成人家的坏事。小人则正好相反。"

Translation:

The Master says, "A gentleman promotes the fortune, not the misfortune, of others. The vulgarian does the opposite."

新 解

君子希望自己好,也希望别人好,总是鼓励别人前进。看到别人有过失则规劝、开导,使之改过;而小人则有嫉妒之心,不希望别人超过自己,常常掩盖别人的缺点并引诱其犯错,陷人于恶。

Contemporary interpretation:

A gentleman wishes that he himself could make progress. He also wishes that others could make progress as well. When seeing the mistakes and shortcomings of others, he is not hesitant to point

九、处 世（Conducting Oneself in Society）

them out and sincerely wishes that they could become perfect. But a mean person will just do the opposite. He does not wish to see that others are better than him in any aspect. When he find others' mistakes and shortcomings, he will not point them out and might even secretly encourage the others to develop their bad habits or commit blunders so as to have them trapped in an irreparable bad situation.

---

12. 子曰："君子和而不同，小人同而不和。"

今 译

孔子说："君子和谐相处但不盲目苟同，小人盲目苟同却不能和谐相处。"

Translation:

The Master says, "The gentleman seeks harmony, not conformity; the vulgarian, conformity, not harmony."

新 解

君子做事有原则，能够处理好矛盾和意见，而自己的原则不会改变；小人则不同，他们多从自己的角度出发，排除异己。即便是赞同自己理念的人，到了利害关头，也容易产生利益冲突，就不能融洽相处。协调关系也是现代工作、人际关系中的一个重要内容。一同共事，有时候看法难免不同，只要能够坦率、诚恳地提出来加以解决就好。相反，如果一味盲从附和，非但不能达到真正的协调，反而会误事。

Contemporary interpretation:

Gentlemen have their living principles. They could negotiate different opinions and viewpoints without compromising their own principles. Mean people are quite different. They deal with everything in light of their own interest. When their own interest is at stake, they will never compromise and will blackball any opposition, thus causing strife and discord. Actually, coordinating relations between people has become one of the important disciplines in our modern life. It is quite natural that people working together may have different points of view towards the same thing. Candor and compromise will resolve any conflict. Unprincipled conformity may actually exacerbate the situation.

---

13. 子贡问曰："乡人皆好之，何如？"子曰："未可也。""乡人皆恶之，何如？"子曰："未可也。不如乡人之善者好之，其不善者恶之。"

九、处 世（Conducting Oneself in Society）

今 译

子贡问道："全乡的人都喜欢他，这个人怎么样？"孔子说："还不可下结论。"子贡又问："全乡人都厌恶他，这个人怎么样？"孔子说："还不可下结论。最好是全乡的好人都喜欢他，全乡的坏人都厌恶他。"

Translation:

Zigong asks the Master, "What do you think of a person liked by all his neighbors?" The Master replies, "It's hard to judge." Zigong asks again, "If a person is disliked by all of the people in the vicinity? What do you think of him?" The Master replies, "It is difficult to make a judgment, too. A really good person should be liked by all the good people and disliked by all of the bad people in the neighborhood."

新 解

孔子认为仅凭群众对于一个人的善恶是很难判断的，有时候群众认为不对的，不一定真的不对；群众认为好的，也不一定真的好。可见，当我们听到群众的意见时，要进行深入分析，问个究；而不要偏听偏信，笼统对待。孔子的话说得很科学，在今天待人接物中也可以借鉴。

Contemporary interpretation:

In Confucius' opinion, it is not safe to judge a person only by his reputation among the people around him, because there are chances when the majority's opinions of a person are not objective. This statement of Confucius indicates that fair judgment of a person calls for a careful interpretation of others' reactions to him. This Confucian teaching about judging a person is still applicable today in our life.

> 14. 或曰："以德报怨，何如？"子曰："何以报德？以直报怨，以德报德。"

今 译

有人说："以恩惠来报答怨恨，这样如何？"孔子说："那么要以什么来报答恩惠呢？应该以正直来报答怨恨，以恩惠来报答恩惠。"

Translation:

Somebody asks the Master, "What do you think of repaying evil with goodness?" The Master replies, "If you repay evil with goodness, then how do you repay goodness? The idea is wrong. You should repay evil with justice, and repay goodness with goodness."

新 解

以德报德，这是应该的。而以德报怨，则无疑是是非恩怨不分的表现。这对有恩于你的人岂不是不公平吗？以怨报怨，

九、处 世 (Conducting Oneself in Society)

冤冤相报何时了？孔子主张要以直报怨，对待于己有怨的人应正直对待，大公无私，该批评就批评，该肯定就肯定。仁者要有原则，明辨是非，既敢爱也敢恨。

Contemporary interpretation:

It is recommendable that we should repay goodness with goodness. As for the idea of repaying evil with goodness, it is opposed by the Master for it shows a person's inability to tell the right from the wrong and will be unfair to those who have been good to us. Surely, Confucius does not advocate repaying evil with evil for that will cause ceaseless cycles of revenge and counter-revenge. But he does not advocate forgiving blindly neither. In Confucius' opinion, we should fairly treat those who have done us bad things. When criticism is necessary, we should not skimp it. And when punishment is necessary, we should not spare it. A noble person should have the quality to tell the right from the wrong and the gut to love and hate.

15. 子曰："可与言而不与言，失人；不可与言而与之言，失言。知者不失人，亦不失言。"

今 译

孔子说："可以同他谈话却不去同他谈话，这样就错过了人；不可以同他谈话却去同他谈话，这样就白费了言语。明智的人

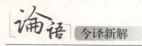

既不错过人,也不白费言语。"

Translation:

The Master says, "When the conversation could be fruitful and yet you choose not to converse with the person, you lose the opportunity of the communicant. When the conversation could not be fruitful, yet you choose to converse with the person, you lose the opportunity of the communication. The wise practices neither."

新 解

说话是人们沟通思想与情意的主要媒介,有智慧的人说话要看对象,要把握言与不言的尺度,要不失人,也不失言。对某些人,该说的要说,哪怕朋友当时听了不谅解。而某些人,不值得对他谈,却硬要谈,不但浪费口舌,而且会得罪人。生活中,唯有做到有知人之明,并能知言,才能结交益友,互相启迪,也才能分辨损友,洁身自爱。

Contemporary interpretation:

Conversation works as one of the major media to facilitate communication between people. Wise people know how to choose the subjects speak to. They know when to speak and when to keep silent. They never speak randomly with those who can not understand them, nor do they lose the chance to converse with those who can understand them. A person, only if he is wise enough to spot a worthy interlocutor can he make beneficial friends and avoid detrimental ones.

九、处 世（Conducting Oneself in Society）

16. 子曰："君子矜而不争，群而不党。"

今 译

孔子说："君子庄矜而不争执，合群而不结党营私。"

Translation:

The Master says, "The gentleman is dignified but not contentious; gregarious, but not cliquish."

新 解

孔子提出了君子修身的两条原则，一是自尊自重而不争名夺利，二是平易近人，不搞宗派，对人一视同仁。

Contemporary interpretation:

Here Confucius suggests two principles for the gentleman. One, he should practice dignity and avert avarice for fame and possessions. Two, he should be amiable and just, and avoid participation in any faction.

17. 子曰："君子不以言举人，不以人废言。"

今 译

孔子说："君子不因为他说得好就举荐他，不因为他人不好就否定他说的话。"

Translation:

The Master says, "The noble does not exalt a person for his volubility, not does he belittle the speech of a person for his bad reputation."

新 解

君子观察人是重实际，不能因为他能说会道就举荐他，一定要听其言观其行，从实际品德、学问出发来推举人，重行而不重言。另一方面，也不因为对方某一点不好就否定他的好意见。说得好不一定有德，无德的人说的话也不一定句句都错。

Contemporary interpretation:

A noble person pays much more attention on observing what a person does instead of on noticing what he says. He will not recommend somebody to a position only because he has a glib tongue. His principle for making a recommendation is to examine the person's virtues and learning. On the other hand, he will play a fair game. He will not rashly negate a person's reasonable opinions

九、处　世（Conducting Oneself in Society）

only because the person has a bad reputation. To put it in a nutshell, a person who utters fine words does not necessarily possess high virtue, and a person without high virtue does not necessarily utter unreasonable words.

---

18. 子曰："众恶之，必察焉；众好之，必察焉。"

今译

孔子说："如果一个人，人人都厌恶他，就一定要考察。如果人人都喜欢他，也一定要考察。"

Translation:

The Master says, "A person, either liked by all or disliked by all, must be examined carefully."

新解

任用人才是政治当中极重要的大事。如果大家都厌恶或喜欢一个人，未必一定可靠。恶人会哗众取宠，通过使用各种手段获得好评。而好人的善行也不一定会被众人了解。因此，在对待人才的问题上，必须谨慎考核，经过实际调查，实事求是，万不可人云亦云。

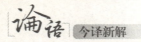

Contemporary interpretation:

Personnel employment is crucial for effective government. A person, either liked by all or disliked by all, is questionable, for a wicked person might camouflage his wickedness by various means and obtain an affirmative evaluation of the others, and a virtuous person might remain unknown by others because of his willing to keep a low profile. In other words, popularity is not a reliable indicator of a person's character, as popularity may favor the ostensible insinuation of the wicked, but not the retiring modesty of the virtuous. Therefore, effective employment of officials is not a matter of popularity competition, but depends on careful examination of the person's actual credentials.

---

19. 子曰:"过而不改,是谓过矣。"

今 译

孔子说:"有了过错却不改正,这就真是过错了!"

Translation:

The Master says, "A mistake that remains uncorrected is the real mistake."

九、处 世（Conducting Oneself in Society）

新 解

每个人都会犯错，有了错误不要紧，能改过就好。有的人知错就改，吃一堑长一智，以后不会再犯同样的错误，自然就进步了。而有的人有过错却不肯改正，反而寻找各种借口，文过饰非，这就是真正的过错了，将来必定会酿成更大的祸患。

Contemporary interpretation:

To err is human. What matters is not the mistake, but the refusal to correct the mistake. Progress and success certainly come from taking lessons from mistakes. Embellishment of mistakes with excuses is latent with catastrophic results.

20. 子曰："当仁，不让于师。"

今 译

孔子说："应当以仁为己任的时候，连老师也不必谦让。"

Translation:

The Master says, "Virtue yields to none, not even to the teacher."

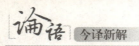

新 解

孔子把仁提到更高层次加以发挥，勉励人要切实为仁。在我国，讲究师道尊严。弟子应恭顺师。但在"为仁"面前，却可以当仁不让。希腊哲学家亚里士多德也说过类似的话："吾爱吾师，吾更爱真理。""当仁不让"这句成语已为人们广泛使用，表示应该做的事，就要积极主动地去做，绝不能推诿。

Contemporary interpretation:

Confucius puts performance of virtue above anything else. In China, the teacher's dignity is time-honored and unchallengeable. Yet even against the dignity of the teacher, virtue has to remain uncompromised. This statement of Confucius is synonymous with Aristotle's dictum "I love my teacher, but I love truth more." The contemporary idiom, "Virtue does not compromise," again teaches that practice of virtue is everyone's personal obligation which should not be shirked.

---

21. 子曰："道不同，不相为谋。"

今 译

孔子说："所走道路不同，就不必相互谋虑了。"

九、处 世（Conducting Oneself in Society）

Translation:

The Master says, "People separate in their courses need not counsel or collaborate with each other."

新 解

交友、谋事要谨慎小心。志同道合，才能共谋大事。思想目的不同，没有办法共同相谋，干脆各行其道，不要谋求谁服从谁。面对那些没有共同目标的人，如果没有办法讨论一件事，又何必勉强合作呢？

Contemporary interpretation:

A person must be very cautious in making friends or choosing colleagues. If he is to form a corporate body and accomplish something great, he must choose those who have the same aspirations, goals and views to work with. Since collaboration among people who do not share common philosophies and aspirations is futile, it's advisable in this case for everyone to follow their separate course.

22. 子曰："乡原，德之贼也。"

今 译

孔子说："不分是非的好好先生，是败坏道德风气的小人。"

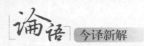

Translation:

The Master says, "A person who offends none is the anathema of virtue."

新 解

乡原是指那些好好先生，他们不分是非，谁都不得罪，做事的时候把自己的责任推得干干净净，处事圆滑而心中毫无理想，这种人令人厌恶。

Contemporary interpretation:

In real life, there are some people who never air their true opinions or make a fair judgment when they are asked to do so. Their principle is to offend nobody and shoulder no responsibility. Such oleaginous people are hypocritical and detesting.

---

23. 子曰："道听而涂说，德之弃也。"

今 译

孔子说："在路上听到一点传说就随便四处传播，这是道德所鄙弃的。"

九、处 世（Conducting Oneself in Society）

Translation:

The Master says, "Virtue despises propagation of hearsay."

新 解

不管是读书做学问，还是为人处世，都不可道听途说，都要深入调查，以事实为依据，不能相信传闻，更不可随便下结论。

Contemporary interpretation:

Whatever we do, we must guard against believing and passing on rumors. Any of our conclusions, be it in scholarship or in human affairs, must be based on founded investigations rather than on alleged rumors.

---

24. 子路曰："君子尚勇乎？"子曰："君子义以为上。君子有勇而无义为乱；小人有勇而无义为盗。"

今 译

子路说："君子推崇勇敢吗？"孔子说："君子推崇的是道义，君子光有勇敢而没有道义，就会作乱；小人光有勇敢而没有道义，就会偷盗。"

Translation:

Zilu asks the Master, "Does the gentleman espouse bravery?" The Master replies, "The gentleman's first espousal is righteousness. If a gentleman has bravery but not righteousness, he might start a riot. If a mean person has bravery but not righteousness, he might become a robber."

新 解

孔子是主张勇敢的,但是君子应具备知、仁、勇三种美德。君子只有勇敢而没有道义的节制就会挑起祸乱,小人只有勇敢没有道义就会铤而走险。所以,正义是衡量是非的标准。

Contemporary interpretation:

Though Confucius upholds bravery, the gentleman needs to possess the triumvirate of knowledge, benevolence, and bravery. Bravery unguided by virtue may make a person riotous or reckless. Virtue arbitrates between the right and the wrong.

---

25. 子曰:"君子周而不比,小人比而不周。"

今 译

孔子说:"君子能在道义上团结人,但不以私情互相勾结;

九、处 世 (Conducting Oneself in Society)

小人善于拉拢人却不会在道义上团结人。"

Translation:

The Master says, "A gentleman is catholic and no partisan. A mean person is a partisan and not catholic."

新 解

这里讨论了君子和小人政治品德的区别。君子在实际处理人际关系中,能够与多数人友好相处,与多数人联合,为公共利益团结一致;而小人则不同,他们与少数人拉帮结派、互相勾结,常因一点小利而破坏大局。

Contemporary interpretation:

Through this statement Confucius made a distinction between the gentleman's political morality and that of the mean person. In dealing with people, the gentleman could get along well with the majority of them. What he concerns about is the interest of the majority. In contrast, the mean person is keen on forming a clique with his like. When the occasion rises, he even dares to destroy a great cause for petty personal gains.

十、为 政（Administration）

> 1. 子曰："道千乘之国，敬事而信，节用而爱人，使民以时。"

今 译

孔子说："治理具有千乘兵车的国家，谨慎处事而守信，节约有度而爱民，役使民众不违时。"

Translation:

The Master says, "To administer a country with one thousand military chariots, one needs to follow three principles: prudent and trustable, frugal and amiable, considerate and caring."

新 解

这一章讲述孔子治理国家的基本原则。孔子有"重民"思

十、为 政（Administration）

想，认为为政者正确处理同民众的关系至关重要，主张施德于民，实行仁政。他提出：一、认真做事，取信于民。对待政事要严肃认真，要有"敬事"精神；对老百姓要讲信用，这样才能站住脚。二、节用爱民。要求为政者要有爱民之德，同情百姓，采取利民政策，减轻人民负担；三、不违农时。劳役要避开农时，使人民安居乐业。

Contemporary interpretation:

Here Confucius states his basic thought about administration of a country. In Confucius' opinion, people are the most important element in a society. To build a harmonious society, the governors must deftly handle their relations with the people. Effective governance must be virtuous and clement. He puts forth three principles: firstly, the governors must be conscientious and work hard to earn trust of the people; secondly, they must enforce policies of frugality to relieve the people of their heavy burdens; and thirdly, they must avoid recruiting farmers in farming seasons and help them to live a happy life.

2. 子曰："为政以德，譬如北辰，居其所而众星共之。"

今 译

孔子说："用德行来治理国政，如同北极星处在自己的位置上而众多的星辰拱卫它。"

Translation:

The Master says, "A country administered with virtue is like the Polestar centered around by other stars."

新 解

孔子认为治理国政要把道德教育放在第一位。他认为只有以"德"教化百姓，百姓才会服从，才能万众一心。这也就是"无为而治"。其实，"无为而治"不是什么都不管，而是"无为无不为"。孔子之所以提倡"德政"，是因为当时社会非常动荡、混乱，权利的争夺十分激烈、残酷；文化教育衰败，世风日下，民不聊生。孔子忧心如焚，因此，他认为：为政，仅靠权利是不够的，只有用"德"教化人民，教化社会，才能从根本上解决问题，才能拯救社会。

Contemporary interpretation:

Confucius thinks that morals and virtues should be put in top priority when the matter of administering a country is concerned. In his opinion, the populace, when educated and moved by morals and virtues possessed by the governors, will love and support their government heart and soul. This is just what is meant "to govern without law" by Confucius. What must be made clear here is that "to govern without law" does not mean sitting idly in the office and doing nothing. The prerequisite of "to govern without law" is to have found the crux of the governing problem and have it resolved

十、为　政（Administration）

in advance. The reason why Confucius puts much emphasis on administering with virtue lies in the riotous and disorderly society at that time. And such a time, Confucius strongly believe, a nation could only become stable and prosperous under government with morals and virtues. Political power and despotism would lead to nowhere.

> 3. 子曰："道之以政，齐之以刑，民免而无耻。道之以德，齐之以礼，有耻且格。"

今　译

孔子说："用政令来教导，用刑法来整治，民众苟免刑罚但缺乏廉耻；用德行来教导，用礼仪来整治，民众知廉耻而且敬服。"

Translation:

The Master says, "Disciplining by means of orders and managing by means of laws may cause people to stay free from legal punishment but not from moral collapse; in contrast, disciplining by means of morals and managing by means of decorum will beware people of the shameful and teach them to practice reverence."

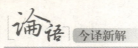

新 解

孔子的"道之以德"的主张构成了他的"德治"理论。孔子的"德治"理论是中国古代治理国家的基本方略,其主要特点就是特别重视民心向背对于国家治理的根本作用。如何才能赢得民心?孔子认为,单用政令、刑法来治民虽然有效,却不能使百姓从内心里拥戴你。要真正获得百姓拥护,必须以道德教育来贯穿始终,以德取心,以德服人。

Contemporary interpretation:

The idea of "educating and guiding people with virtue" constitutes the essence of Confucius' "governing with virtue" theory, which is the basic strategy by ancient Chinese monarchs in administering their nations. The theory is characterized by its emphasis on public sentiment and its impact on governance of the country. According to Confucius, orders and laws are effective in managing people, but they can not make people respect and support the managers heart and soul. If the rulers expect the mass people to support them sincerely, they must spent much time and energy instilling morals and virtues into the minds of their people, and first and foremost, they themselves must be the epitomes of morals and virtues.

4. 季康子问政于孔子。孔子对曰:"政者,正也。子帅以正,孰敢不正?"

十、为　政（Administration）

今 译

季康子问孔子如何治理国家。孔子回答说："政就是正的意思。您自己带头走正路，那么还有谁敢不走正道呢？"

Translation:

Counseled on statecraft by Ji Kang, the Master replies, "Administration is synonymous with righteousness. If you the administrator take the lead choosing the righteous path, who dares to take the opposite way?"

新 解

孔子认为当政就要以身作则，为政者在行动中要起表率作用。所谓"上梁不正下梁歪"，指的是统治者的身教重于言教。要端正别人的行为，先要端正自己，自己行为端正了，才能教育别人不越轨。所以提高自己的道德修养，起模范带头作用，是治理好国家的根本之道。

Contemporary interpretation:

Confucius contends that the administrators themselves must set up an example for their subordinates and the mass people to follow. Just as the Chinese saying puts it, "When the upper beam is crooked, the lower one will go askew." It teaches that practice of the preach influences more effectively than the preach itself. Only when the administrators' behaviors are in keeping with morals and laws, do they have the qualification to educate and guide the mass people. Therefore, the governors' paragon of their own virtue and morality should be the fundamental strategy to govern a country.

---

5. 子曰:"其身正,不令而行;其身不正,虽令不从。"

今 译

孔子说:"执政人行为端正,不发布命令,人们也会执行;自身的行为不端正,即使三令五申,人们也不会听从。"

Translation:

The Master says, "An upright governor gains compliance without use of the decree; a crooked governor wins no compliance despite decrees."

新 解

孔子认为政令能否得以推行主要在于执政人的行为。任何一种制度,到底还是人为的,个人的修养非常重要。一些掌握政权的人,只知制定种种法规,可是本身行为不正,法规再多,人民哪里会听从你呢?"正人先正己",这是为国当政者的一个先决条件。要求别人做到的,自己首先要做到。领导者如果不能以身作则,对政事的治理就不会有效。

十、为 政 (Administration)

Contemporary interpretation:

In Confucius' opinion, whether a governor's orders could be readily accepted and followed by the governed or not depends on the governor's personal behaviors. Every edict, written or oral, is to be carried out by the people. If the governor himself is not upright, he should not feel shocked at his decrees being rejected by the people. Actually, we could consider the advocacy "Rectifying oneself before rectifying others" as the prerequisite for being a governor. The governor must take the lead in conducting himself. If he fails to set an example for the people, his decrees naturally will not be effectively implemented.

---

6. 季康子患盗，问于孔子。孔子对曰："苟子之不欲，虽赏之不窃。"

今 译

季康子苦于盗贼太多，向孔子求教。孔子答道："如果你自己不贪求财货，即使奖励偷盗，他们也不会去偷。"

Translation:

Ji Kang was troubled by burglars. He asked the Master about the solution. The Master says, "If you, sir, were not covetous, they would not steal even rewarded."

新解

社会风气总是上行下效的，如果统治者都贪得无厌，有些人迫于生计或上行下效，就会沦为盗贼。在这句话里孔子强调，如果统治者能自身廉洁，以德化民，即使鼓励为盗，百姓也会知耻而不愿为盗。孔子之言至今仍有强大的生命力。

Contemporary interpretation:

The inferior emulates what the superior does. Avarice by the latter will turn the former, when poor, into thieves. Here Confucius points out the importance of being a clean governor and building a clean government. If the country is governed with virtue and morality, the people living in it will not steal a thread even rewarded, because they know that stealing is a shameful thing. Confucius' words are still meaningful and thought-evoking today.

---

7. 季康子问政于孔子曰："如杀无道，以就有道，何如？"孔子对曰："子为政，焉用杀？子欲善而民善矣。君子之德风，小人之德草，草上之风，必偃。"

今译

季康子向孔子问怎么样治理国家，说："如果杀掉无道的

十、为 政（Administration）

人来成全有道的人，怎么样？"孔子答道："治理国家，哪里用得着杀戮的手段呢？只要你向善，百姓也就会向善。身在高位的人的品德好比风，百姓的品德好比草。风吹到草上，草一定会随风倒下的。"

Translation:

Ji Kang asked Confucius about the way to govern a country, saying, "What about killing those who are lawless to protect those who are law-abiding?" Confucius replies, "What's the use of slaughter in governing a country? If you pursue goodness, the people will follow suit. The virtue of a governor is like the wind, and the virtue of the people is like the grass. The grass bends the way the wind above it blows."

新 解

孔子把当权者的品德比作风，把百姓的品德行为比作草，风朝哪边刮，草就向哪边倒。说明道德风气的好坏问题不在百姓，关键在于当权者正身、修德。

Contemporary interpretation:

By the analogy Confucius points out that the trend of social morality is not determined by the mass people, but by the governors. Their virtues and uprightness are very important in shaping social morality.

8. 子曰:"上好礼,则民易使也。"

今 译

孔子说:"在上位的人重视礼,那么百姓就好指挥了。"

Translation:

The Master says, "When the ruler espouses decorum and propriety, the ruled will readily comply."

新 解

这里讲的也是统治者自己要先作出表率,以礼治国,百姓就会拥护你,自然就按你的要求加倍努力了。

Contemporary interpretation:

The statement indicates that if the rulers could take the lead observing the rules of propriety and govern with virtue people will not spare their efforts to support the rulers.

9. 子适卫,冉有仆。子曰:"庶矣哉!"冉有曰:"既庶矣,又何加焉?"曰:"富之。"曰:"既富矣,又何加焉?"曰:"教之。"

十、为 政（Administration）

今 译

孔子到卫国去，冉有给他赶车。孔子说："人口真多呀！"冉有说："人口已经够多了，还要再做些什么呢？"孔子说："使他们富起来。"冉有说："富了以后还要做些什么呢？"孔子说："对他们进行教化。"

Translation:

The Master was visiting the State of Wei, and Ran You was attending the Master by driving the chariot himself. The Master says, "What a dense population!" Ran You replies, "The population is large enough, what more should be done for them?" The Master replies, "Enrich them." Ran You asks once more, "And then?" The Master replies, "Enlighten them."

新 解

这篇对话记载了孔子"先富后教"的主张。孟子、荀子也都把这一主张继续发挥。庶、富、教，是孔子治国的三项目标。庶，指人口众多。古代地广人稀，使国家人口众多是治国的首要大事；富，就是让百姓富起来。教，就是要进行道德教化。在人口增长之后，孔子认为必须让人民富裕起来，富裕之后则要进行文化、礼仪教育，以提高人民的道德水平。光富不教，就会贪婪而不知廉耻。繁荣、富有、文化教育，是政治发展的三阶段。

Contemporary interpretation:

This conversation reveals Confucius' idea of "Enriching

people before enlightening them." After Confucius, both Mencius and Master Xun had further elaborated on the idea. "Populating, enriching and enlightening" are three goals of Confucius' governing concept. In ancient times, the vast land was usually sparsely-populated. Therefore, an ample population was a crucial issue. The governor's second goal was wealth for the people. And then he should make the virtues and morality prevail across the rich country. People without virtue and morality are prone to greed and shame. In a nutshell, populating, enriching and enlightening should be understood as three stages along which a state is supposed to develop.

---

10. 哀公问于有若曰:"年饥,用不足,如之何?"有若对曰:"盍彻乎?"曰:"二,吾犹不足,如之何其彻也?"对曰:"百姓足,君孰与不足?百姓不足,君孰与足?"

今 译

鲁哀公问有若说:"遭了饥荒,国家用度不足,怎么办呢?"有若回答说:"何不实行彻法,只抽十分之一的田租呢?"哀公说:"现在抽十分之二,我还不够,怎么能实行彻法呢?"有若回答说:"百姓富足了,国君怎么会用度不足?百姓贫困,

十、为 政（Administration）

国君又怎么会用度充足呢？"

Translation:

Duke Ai asks You Ruo, "It is a year of dearth, and the state has not enough for its needs. What am I to do?" You Ruo replies, "Have you not got your tithes?" The Duke says, "Even with two-tenths instead of one, I still do not have enough. What is the use of talking to me about tithes?" You Ruo says, "When the people are rich, the king will not suffer from the pinch. When the people are needy, how could the king have plenty?"

新 解

富国应先使百姓富足起来，民富而后国强，这才是富国之本。

Contemporary interpretation:

A country will become prosperous and powerful only after its people have become rich. This is the fundamental principle in enriching a country.

---

11. 子贡问政。子曰："足食，足兵，民信之矣。"子贡曰："必不得已而去，于斯三者何先？"曰："去兵。"子贡曰："必不得已而去，于斯二者何先？"曰："去食。自古皆有死，民无信不立。"

今 译

子贡问怎样治理政事。孔子说:"要使粮食充足,军备充足,百姓信任政府。"子贡说:"如果不得不去掉一项,那么在这三项中先去哪一项呢?"孔子说:"去掉军备。"子贡说:"如果不得不再去掉一项,那么在剩下的两项中先去哪一项呢?"孔子说:"去掉粮食。自古以来人总是要死的,但是如果百姓没有了信念,国家就不能存在。"

Translation:

Zigong asks the Master about the art of government. The Master says, "The government must have ample provisions, enough men and arms, and people's faith in it." Zigong asks, "If one among the three requirements must be sacrificed, which one do you think should be relinquished first?" The Master replies, "Men and arms." Zigong asks once more, "If one more is to be omitted, which one should that be?" The Master replies, "Provisions. As you know, from time immemorial death has been the lot of all men, but if the people have no faith in their rulers, there is no standing of the state."

新 解

孔子认为国家的基础建立在充足的粮食、军备和人民的信念三个要素上,其中以人民的信念最为重要。国家军事力量强大,经济富足发达,人民自然就会对政府有信心。但是,如果一个国家完全没有军备和粮食,其人民只能饿死或被敌

十、为　政（Administration）

人杀死，却要求人民信任它或对它有信心，似乎太不合情理了。因此，孔子的意思应该是，即使国家的军备、粮食已尽，而这个国家的人民却是一个有信念乃至有信仰的、顶天立地的民族，那么国家还是可以依赖于他们重新建立起来。古往今来，许多失去民心的政府都以垮台而告终。为政者必须记住"民无信不立"的告诫，一定要取信于民，才能繁荣昌盛，国富民强。

Contemporary interpretation:

In Confucius' opinion, a country should be solidly based on the three elements of ample food provisions, enough men and arms, and people's strong confidence in the government. Among the three elements, people's confidence in the government is the most important. And this element will naturally follow when the country is prosperous and powerful. Undeniably, in an impoverished country where the people are either plagued by famines or slaughtered by enemies, the rulers have no right to require people's confidence in them. But what Confucius intends to convey is that even though a country might be in dire need of food and men and arms, so long as the people have a strong faith in their government and belief in themselves, the country may gain its standing again. Throughout history, many a government, to which the people gave no confidence, had ended up in collapse. So the governors today must take the lessons and remember that without people's confidence the government will not last for long, and that only when the people are confident in them can the country become prosperous and powerful.

> 12. 叶公问政。子曰:"近者说,远者来。"

今 译

叶公问怎样管理政事。孔子说:"使近处的人高兴,远方的人归附。"

Translation:

The duke of Ye asks the Master about government. The Master says, "Good government pleases those that are near and attracts those that are far."

新 解

"近者说,远者来"是孔子的政治理想。也就是说,要得到百姓的拥护。对领导人来说,跟随的人不愿离开,在外面的人都想回来,别处的人都想来投效,这就是成功的领导艺术。在外交上,能够与临近的国家和睦相处,与相距遥远的国家友好交往,这就是成功的外交关系。

Contemporary interpretation:

"To make those who are near happy and those who are far off attracted" is a political ideal of Confucius. This thought of

十、为 政（Administration）

Confucius still applies to contemporary government and diplomacy. Competent government enjoys strong followership and draws to itself all people, near and far. Competent diplomacy achieves amity with neighboring nations and successful connections with distant ones.

十一、教 育（Education）

1. 子曰："温故而知新，可以为师矣。"

今 译

孔子说："温习旧知识，学习知识，就能成为老师了。"

Translation:

The Master says, "One that continuously reviews his old knowledge and learns the new can be a good teacher."

新 解

"温故知新"从学习的角度来看，强调了"复习"的作用。人的记忆是有限的，只有不断地巩固学过的知识，并且在温习的过程中发现新的问题，这样的学习方法才会事半功倍。"温故知新"从为政的角度看，含有"前事不忘，后事之师"的意

十一、教　育（Education）

思。前面的成功与失败，历史会如实地告诉你，只有善于总结研究，师法过去，才能准确判断未来新事物的发展方向。

Contemporary interpretation:

Applied to learning, this Confucian precept stresses the importance of reviewing already-learnt knowledge, so dictated by the finite human capacity in memory. Review of old knowledge is important as it may produce new serendipities. Looked at from the perspective of administering, this statement has the same implication as the saying "Past experience, if not forgotten, may serve as a guide for the future." History is a mirror. It can faithfully reflect the successes and failures in the past. A person, only on condition that he could draw lessons from the history, can accurately judge the direction at which things are developing.

2. 子曰：“《诗》三百，一言以蔽之，曰：'思无邪。'”

今　译

孔子说：“《诗》三百篇，用一句话来概括，就是思想纯正。”

Translation:

The Master says, "The pith of poems in the *Book of Poetry*,

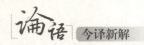

though three hundred in number, is 'Think no evil'."

新 解

孔子概括《诗经》的主旨是"思无邪",并非讨论《诗经》本身,而是指出为政与文学的关系,用诗教来陶冶人的思想,强调"诗言志",认为《诗经》有"兴、观、群、怨"的作用。他的这些看法对后世影响很大。

Contemporary interpretation:

What Confucius discusses here seemingly concerns the principal theme of the *Book of Poetry*, but actually alluding to the relationship between administration and literature. In Confucius' opinion, literary works such as the *Book of Poetry* "express the ideal" and function to educate the person and edify the mind. This opinion of Confucius has exerted a great influence on post-Confucian literature and generations.

> 3. 子曰:"吾十有五而志于学,三十而立,四十而不惑,五十而知天命,六十而耳顺,七十而从心所欲,不逾矩。"

今 译

孔子说:"我十五岁有志于学习,三十岁自立,四十岁不

十一、教　育（Education）

疑惑，五十岁了解天命，六十岁听到什么都能领悟，七十岁随心所欲而不逾越法度。"

Translation:

The Master says, "At fifteen I had my mind bent on learning. At thirty, I had become established. At forty, I no longer suffered from perplexities. At fifty, I knew the decrees of Heaven. At sixty, I heard them with a docile and discerning ear. At seventy, I followed what my heart desires without transgressing the bounds of rightness."

新　解

此章是孔子自述修身的人生进程。孔子认为必须经过从自律到自觉的飞跃，才能达到修养的最高境界。在人生的旅途上，每一个不同的年龄段里我们有着不同的特征和目标。孔子用这样简洁的话语概括了一种理想、规整的人生状态。每一个人都要经历少年时的意气风发、青年时的艰苦求索、壮年时的平和沉稳、老年时的洒脱超然。贯穿始终的是积极的心态和对人伦道德法则的遵循。孔子在这里向世人提供了一种有指导性的、有轨迹可循的人生道路。

Contemporary interpretation:

This statement is Confucius' account of his progressive self-cultivation. According to Confucius, a person must undergo the self-discipline to self volition process before he reaches the apex self refinement. Different aims and attitudes characterize different steps along the way of personal growth. In pithy language, Confucius encapsulates the steps of an ideal and consummate life: ebullience at adolescence; exploration at youth, equanimity at midlife, and insouciance at the old age. Thematic to this life is active practice of virtue, as reflected in the guiding trajectory proffered by Confucius.

---

4. 子曰:"默而识之,学而不厌,诲人不倦,何有于我哉!"

今 译

孔子说:"默默记住所学的内容,勤奋学习不感到厌烦,教导别人不感到疲倦,这三件事对于我又有什么难的呢?"

Translation:

The Master says, "I have been silently remembering, insatiably learning and untiringly teaching knowledge. These at least are merits which I can confidently claim."

新 解

"默而识之"是说做学问不可心存外务,默默领会在心是最要紧的;"学而不厌"是说做学问的兴趣要长久不减;"诲人

十一、教　育（Education）

不倦"是说教育人要不知疲倦。这三点正是孔子学习和教学的原则，都是通过自身努力就可以做到的。

Contemporary interpretation:

By "silently remembering" Confucius means that a person should be engrossed in his learning. By "insatiably learning" he means that a person should learn all his life. By "untiringly teaching" he means that a person should impart his knowledge to others with patience. These are three principles by which Confucius learns and teaches.

5. 子曰："德之不修，学之不讲，闻义不能徙，不善不能改，是吾忧也。"

今　译

孔子说："道德不培养，学问不讲习，听到义却不追求，知道自己的不足却不改正，这是我的几大忧虑啊！"

Translation:

The Master says, "Here are my four concerns: failure to cultivate virtue, failure to discuss what is just studied, failure to pursue righteousness, and failure to reform my own faults."

新 解

孔子所忧的"修德"、"讲学"、"迁善"、"改过"四件事,实质是提出了个人的道德修养问题。人不可能没有缺点,只要"知过必改",加强思想锻炼和修养,就能达到仁人的境界,这是针对时弊而发的。在精神文明亟须大力提倡的今天,也应该树立一些简明易懂的标准,孔子提出的这四个方面可以作为一种参考。

Contemporary interpretation:

The four things worrying Confucius are actually closely related to a person's moral cultivation. No person is flawless. So long as he can revise his mistakes the very moment he realizes it, he will reach the realm of goodness. The statement, though uttered thousands of years ago, is still applicable today in lifting people's virtues and mapping social norms.

6. 子曰:"不愤不启,不悱不发,举一隅不以三隅反,则不复也。"

今 译

孔子说:"不到学生苦苦思索而不得解,我不去启发他;

十一、教　育（Education）

不到他反复默想，要想说出而说不出时，我不去开导他。列举一个道理而不能类推出三个道理，那么在这个问题上我就不再教他了。"

Translation:

The Master says, "Until the student has tried and still fail to understand, I will not enlighten him. Until the student has tried and words still do not come, I will not give him guidance. If I explain something to the student and he cannot draw inferences by analogy, I will not repeat my lesson."

新　解

孔子在教育中实行启发式教学，是有积极意义的。孔子的教学着眼于在教师的主导作用下，诱导学生开动脑筋，充分调动学生学习的主动性、积极性，培养学生独立思考的能力，从而做到触类旁通、举一反三。这样学习的结果，知识必然面广、量大而实在。孔子的这些教育思想和方法，是他长期进行教育实践的经验总结，是我国教育思想宝库中的一份珍贵财富，直到今天仍有实际意义。

Contemporary interpretation:

The enlightening method by which Confucius teaches is of great significance. This teaching concept emphasizes teacher's guiding function and students' learning initiative and thinking competence. It also emphasizes students' competence in making inferences by analogy. In Confucius's opinion, knowledge acquired this way will be solid and extensive. The concept, like a pearl in the treasure-trove of Chinese educational thoughts, is results of Confucius' life-long teaching experience, and is still very meaningful today.

7. 子曰:"爱之,能勿劳乎?忠焉,能勿诲乎?"

今 译

孔子说:"爱他,能不教他勤奋吗?忠于他,能不教诲他吗?"

Translation:

The Master says, "Can there be love which does not demand industry from its object? Can there be loyalty which does not lead to instruction of its object?"

新 解

爱小辈就要让他们从小多吃点苦,以勤养正。"穷人的孩子早当家",从小让孩子养尊处优往往养成孩子好吃懒做的习惯。真正爱孩子就要培养孩子勤俭节约、吃苦耐劳等优良品质,要让他们懂得为人处事的道理,这胜过给他们亿万家财。忠于一个人,不是随声附和,二是谆谆教诲他,使他走正道,这才

十一、教 育 (Education)

是真正的忠。

Contemporary interpretation:

Love for the young should be austere and demanding. According to Confucius, the object of it should suffer some hardships so that he could develop an industrious character. As what is meant by the Chinese saying "A child from a needy family becomes independent earlier than the one from a wealthy family," true love of a child entails fostering his good qualities of industry, frugality, and perseverance. Lavishing the child with love and indulging him in whatever he wishes to eat or to do will only breed bad habits. Cultivation of the way of humanity into a child is better than a bequest of a billion dollars. Genuine loyalty is not complete complaisance to the person, but caring consummation of the person.

8. 子曰："有教无类。"

今 译

孔子说："我对人不加区分，都愿意教育他们。"

Translation:

The Master says, "My teaching discriminates against none."

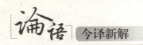

新 解

孔子的时代没有正规的学校,只有贵族或有钱人家的子弟才能学习文化知识。孔子能在等级社会里提出"有教无类"的主张,表现了孔子平等的教育精神,确实难能可贵。孔子是我国历史上第一个办私学的人,打破了官学对学生的限制。他有弟子三千,贤者七十。孔子不分贵贱、地域、贤愚、善恶,只要虚心向学,他一律谆谆教导。孔子被尊为伟大的教育家、至圣先师是当之无愧的。

Contemporary interpretation:

In Confucius' times, there were no regular schools. Only those wealthy families could afford private schooling to their offspring. Therefore, educational opportunities then were unequal. Confucius' "discrimination against none" in education advocates his educational egalitarianism, a precious idea in his own time. Confucius is the first in Chinese history to institute private schooling, breaking the restraint of governmental monopoly over education. His students numbered three thousand, seventy of whom became of saintly distinction. His teaching was open to anyone willing to learn, regardless of their status, location, intelligence, or morality. Confucius certainly deserves the title of "the Great Educator and the Saintly Master."

十一、教 育（Education）

9. 子路问成人。子曰："若臧武仲之知，公绰之不欲，卞庄子之勇，冉求之艺，文之以礼乐，亦可以为成人矣。"曰："今之成人者何必然？见利思义，见危授命，久要不忘平生之言，亦可以为成人矣。"

今 译

子路问孔子什么样的人才算得上完人。孔子说："像臧武仲那样有智慧，孟公绰那样没有贪欲，卞庄子那样勇敢，冉求那样多艺，再加上礼乐修养和文采，也就可以算是一个完人了。"孔子又说："现在的完人何必一定要这样呢。见财利不忘义，遇危难不惧死，久处贫困不食言，也就可以说是完人了。"

Translation:

Zilu asks the Master about the perfect man. The Master replies, "A man, if as knowledgeable as Zang Wuzhong, as content as Meng Gongzhuo, as brave as Zhuangzi of Bian, as polymathic as Ran Qiu, and graced with the refinement of etiquette and music, might be considered as a perfect man." And then he adds, "Nowadays a perfect man needs not to burden himself with these qualities. If he could think of righteousness on seeing gains, could sacrifice life when another is in danger, and could keep his word in poverty, he could be said to be a perfect man."

新 解

孔子谈了自己对怎样才是一个完美无缺的人的看法，那就是智慧、无私、勇敢、多才多艺，还有礼乐修养。然后他也实事求是地提出了较为现实的标准，而且说得十分具体，即能做到见利思义，见危授命，不忘旧约也就很可贵了。可见，孔子的目标是培养人格完善的人，理想的标准是要有智慧，有多种才能，勇敢且没有贪欲；即使退而求其次，也要求有良好的道德修养，能为理想献身，能信守诺言。

Contemporary interpretation:

Here Confucius expresses his viewpoint about a complete man. In his opinion, such a man should be knowledgeable, selfless, courageous, versatile, and refined in rituals and music. In accordance to the reality of his own times, Confucius adapts his standards of the consummate life to make them more realistic and concrete: thought of righteousness at the sight of profit, sacrifice of life when another is in danger, keeping of one's word despite poverty. If falling short of these requirements, a person still needs to strive for moral cultivation, sacrifice for the ideal and preservation of the promise.

10. 子以四教：文、行、忠、信。

今 译

孔子用四种内容教育学生：古代文献，社会实践，忠诚老

十一、教 育（Education）

实，守信遵约。

Translation:

These are the four precepts of the Master: classics, praxis, loyalty, and fidelity.

新 解

这是孔子平日教诲学生必须掌握的立身处世的四项基本纲领。孔子的教学非常注意立身做人，着重教育学生忠诚于事业，取信于朋友，立足于社会。

Contemporary interpretation:

These are four principles by which Confucius instructs his students to live. Confucius' educational thoughts focus on cultivating students' virtues and healthy personalities. He also emphasizes that as a person one should be loyal to his career, trustworthy to his friends and possesses a firm standing in the society.

十二、生 死（Life and Death）

1. 曾子曰："慎终追远，民德归厚矣。"

今 译

曾子说："慎重地办理父母的丧事，追念远代的祖先，人民的道德就会归于淳朴厚道。"

Translation:

Master Zeng says, "Let there be a careful attention to perform the funeral rites to parents, and let sacrifices be offered in memory of the ancestors; then the virtue of the people will resume its pristine purity."

新 解

孝是中华民族的传统美德，又是醇化社会风俗的措施之一。

十二、生 死（Life and Death）

"饮水思源"，我们不能忘记自己的祖先。人类一代代延续相传，没有上一代的开创，就没有这一代的基础；没有这一代的基础，就没有下一代的繁荣。举办丧礼，既是表示对死去的人的追思，提醒我们心存感恩，也是把对于死者的亲情和爱情加以培养和发扬，同时对于活着的人也是一种提示，把死者的接力棒一代代地传递下去。这种做法将有助于减少人与人之间的冲突，能够使社会道德趋于醇厚。

Contemporary interpretation:

Being Filial to parents is a traditional Chinese virtue. It is also a way to purify and moralize social conventions. While enjoying the comforts provided by the society, we should not forget that it is our forefathers who have provided us with these comforts. Without the pioneers' exploration, there won't be a foundation for contemporary and future prosperity. Performing a funeral rite could not only express our lamentation over the death of our parents but also remind us to relay their selfless love to the ensuing generations. In the meantime, it is conducive to cultivaate young people's awareness of gratitude. And this awareness of gratitude, coupled with true love from our hearts, will help to decrease conflicts between people and make social morality resume its proper excellence.

2. 祭如在，祭神如神在。子曰："吾不与祭，如不祭。"

今 译

祭祀祖先,好像祖先真在受祭;祭神,也好像神真在受祭。孔子说:"我如果不能亲自参与祭祀,请人代祭,就好像没有祭过一样。"

Translation:

Offer sacrifices to the ancestor as if in his real presence; offer sacrifices to God as if in God's real presence. The Master says, "Sacrificial offering done in proxy is no sacrificial offering."

新 解

孔子对于祭祀,有"祭神如神在"的诚敬之心。如果只是表面上非常恭敬,内心并不如此,是言行不一的表现,那是没用的。在孔子看来,祭祖如果自己不参加,只是象征性地由别人代表一番,这就等于没祭。可见孔子是非常重视实事求是而反对走形式的。孔子对待祭神的态度,告诉了我们心口如一的做人道理。

Contemporary interpretation:

By "Making a sacrificial offering as if the god were there" Confucius means that while making a sacrificial offering to the deceased one must be very sincere deep down in heart. If one puts an appearance of respect but deep down he is not respectful at all, the sacrificial ceremony amounts to a waste of time and material. Confucius teaches that what the mouth says must match what the

十二、生 死（Life and Death）

heart feels.

> 3. 子不语怪、力、乱、神。

今 译

孔子不谈论怪异、暴力、动乱和鬼神。

Translation:

The Master never speaks of the grotesque, the violent, the riotous, and the preternatural.

新 解

在孔子的思想体系里，他维护正道而不谈论怪异，提倡仁德而不谈强力，主张社会治理有序而不谈叛乱。他重人事轻鬼神。因为怪异、鬼神，玄虚难明；勇力、暴乱，不值得提倡，讲得太多于人无益。孔子也没有明确地说鬼神是不存在的，他对鬼神世界持开放的"存而不论"的态度。孔子更重视解决现实问题。

Contemporary interpretation:

Confucian ideology champions justice, order, and humanity and opposes talking of paranormal phenomena, coercion, disorder and spirits. He believes that too much talk of these negative topics will bring harm to the society. Therefore, people should avoid talking about them. From this statement we could infer that Confucius has not negated the existence of the celestial beings. His attitude towards gods and spirits is neutral, neither affirming nor negating their existence. In his ideological system, dealing with problems existing in reality is much more important than talking about things which are airy and mysterious.

4. 季路问事鬼神。子曰:"未能事人,焉能事鬼?"曰:"敢问死。"曰:"未知生,焉知死?"

今 译

子路问如何事奉鬼神。孔子说:"不能事奉人,怎能事奉鬼呀!""请问死是怎样的?"孔子说:"不知道生,怎么能知道死呢?"

Translation:

Jilu asks how the spirits of the dead and gods should be served. The Master replies, "How can one serve the dead when one cannot even serve the living?" Jilu asks again about death. The Master replies, "How can one know about death if one does not

十二、生 死（Life and Death）

know about life？"

新 解

古人对于生死的认识还是很模糊的，孔子则比较现实，他没有否认鬼神的存在，对鬼神的态度是"敬鬼神而远之"，"未能事人，焉能事鬼"。孔子认为只有知道如何生与为何生，才能明白死的意义。这其实也是孔子在教育学生从现实出发，以人为主，以生为先，切切实实地做学问，追求仁德。

Contemporary interpretation:

The ancient understanding of life and death was nebulous. Confucius knows this and takes a matter-of-fact attitude towards people's belief in gods and spirits, thinking that serving the living should be prior to serving the celestial beings. Understanding of death, Confucius maintains, is impossible without first the understanding of the purpose of life. He instructs his students to start with the living, the real, the knowable, and the virtuous.

十三、孔子其人（Confucius—the Man）

1. 子食于有丧者之侧，未尝饱也。子于是日哭，则不歌。

今 译

孔子在有丧事的人家吃饭，从来没有吃饱过。孔子要是这一天哭过丧，就不会再唱歌。

Translation:

When eating in a bereaved family, the Master never ate his full. If he was a mourner, he would not sing during the whole funeral ceremony.

新 解

古人对于丧礼特别重视。孔子参加丧礼，与人同哀，心存

十三、孔子其人（Confucius—the Man）

哀痛恻隐之心，难过得吃不下饭。当参加丧礼吊祭哭泣后，孔子一天便不再唱歌。可见孔子为人处事都合于礼，而且是个感情丰富、很有同情心的人。

Contemporary interpretation:

Ancient funeral was a solemn ceremony. When attending such a ceremony, Confucius would mourn together with the bereaved, feeling so sad as to lose his appetite. He would refrain from singing during the day of condolences. Clearly a tender-hearted and caring person, the Master conducts himself in strict accordance with decorum.

2. 子在川上曰："逝者如斯夫，不舍昼夜！"

今 译

孔子站在河边说："逝去事物的就好像这河水，不分日夜向前奔流。"

Translation:

The Master once stood by the river side, saying, "What is past is like this; it will go on passing regardless of day and night."

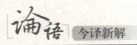

新解

这段话是孔子站在河边,面对滚滚东逝的流水,感叹时光如流水,一去不复返。孔子用这个比喻警示人们要认识自然规律,教育人们效法水之顽强,穿石而过,永不畏难;效法水之有恒,坚持不懈,永远向前;效法水之谦逊、宽广,胸怀博大,永不自满。从而珍惜时间,只争朝夕,自强不息。孔子的话今天读来,更具有现实意义。它教育人们要珍惜时光,发愤忘食,不能有一丝的懈怠,学好文化科学知识,成为社会有用之才。

Contemporary interpretation:

This contemplation was made by Confucius while facing a river running eastward. By this remark Confucius admonished people that life is transient and the passage of time is ineluctable. This Confucian contemplation reminds us that every phenomenon in nature abides by the ceaseless cycle of natural laws; what is bygone is gone forever, only replaced by what is to come. What Confucius implies in his words is still meaningful up to today. It reminds people cherishing time and mastering knowledge so as to be useful to the society.

3. 厩焚。子退朝,曰:"伤人乎?"不问马。

十三、孔子其人（Confucius—the Man）

今 译

马棚着火了，孔子从朝廷回来，知道失火后，问："伤到人了吗？"没有问马怎么样了。

Translation:

When coming back from the court and being told the horse stable had been on fire, the Master asked, "Has anybody been hurt?" He did not ask about the horses.

新 解

马与人比较起来，孔子更关心人，表现了孔子人性关怀的一面。

Contemporary interpretation:

This story reveals Confucius' humanity. Clearly, in his mind, human beings are much more important than beasts.

---

4. 孔子于乡党，恂恂如也，似不能言者。其在宗庙朝庭，便便言，唯谨尔。

今 译

孔子在家乡，温和恭顺，像不会说话的样子。他在宗庙朝

廷,却善于辞令,只是很谨慎。

Translation:

Confucius, in his village, looked humble and simple, as if he were clumsy with words. But in the court and the ancestral temple, he spoke eloquently on every point, though with much caution.

新解

孔子在乡里,不愿夸示自己的本领,没有必要就不多说。这是因为家乡长辈多,孔子以谦逊的态度对待,不愿在长辈面前显露其学问和名声而夸夸其谈。在朝廷、宗庙,由于职务关系,对于有关政事,必须表明自己的态度,所以必须畅言,但说话时,仍持慎重态度。

Contemporary interpretation:

In his hometown, Confucius avoided speaking with his "silver tongue" for he did not want to show off his talent in rhetoric and his profound knowledge in front of the village seniors. This reflects the humble and amiable attitude of Confucius the great man. On the other hand, Confucius would speak eloquently in the court and the ancestral temple because he knew that so far as the duty of an official is concerned, he must fully, though prudently, express himself.

十三、孔子其人（Confucius—the Man）

5. 子入太庙，每事问。或曰："孰谓鄹人之子知礼乎？入太庙，每事问。"子闻之，曰："是礼也。"

今 译

孔子进太庙，每件事情都要问。有人说："谁说叔梁纥的儿子知礼呢？到了太庙，每件事都要问。"孔子听见了，说："这就是礼呀！"

Translation:

When the Master entered the Temple of King Zhou, he consulted the person in charge about every ceremonial procedure. Seeing this, somebody said, "Who said the son of Shu Lianghe knows etiquette? Look, he asks about everything." Hearing this, the Master said, "Isn't the humble enquiry itself etiquette?"

新 解

孔子重视"周礼"并加以弘扬，所以他到了周公庙，虔诚请教。人们误解了他，他说"每事问"就是"礼"。这种对"周礼"谦恭遵循的态度，表现了他虚心好学、不耻下问的精神。我们出国、访友，或者求知、做事都是一样，不要不懂装懂，而要诚恳地向人请教。这就是"礼"的精神，也是做人的道理。

Contemporary interpretation:

Confucius values very much the "Protocol of the Zhou

Dynasty" and is devoted to the propagation of it. Therefore, when he enters the Temple of King Zhou, he behaves very humbly and consults the temple steward about every ceremonial procedure. When misunderstood, he politely says that enquiry about everything itself is a manifestation of etiquette. This story reveals his great respect for the "Protocol of the Zhou Dynasty" and his modesty in learning it. When traveling in a foreign country, visiting a friend, or acquiring knowledge, we should do as Confucius did in the temple, earnestly consulting people around us about what we do not know. This is the essence of etiquette and the way of conducting oneself.

6. 子曰："莫我知也夫！"子贡曰："何为其莫如知子也？"子曰："不怨天，不尤人，下学而上达。知我者其天乎！"

今 译

孔子感叹说："没有人理解我啊。"子贡问道："您没有被人理解的是什么呢？"孔子说："我不怨恨上天的不公，不责怪人世的磨难；居于社会下层，却通过努力的学习而通达了最高的道理。能够理解我的大概只有上天吧。"

十三、孔子其人（Confucius—the Man）

Translation:

The Master exclaims, "Nobody knows about me." Zigong asks, "Why do you say so?" The Master replies, "I blame neither the heavenly being nor the earthly one. Though of an obscure origin, I have acquired the sublime knowledge through learning. It may well be that only the Supreme Being will know me."

新 解

孔子出身穷困，在艰难困苦的环境下，他不怨天尤人，通过后天努力不懈地学习与求索，成就了智慧的德业。他这种身处逆境自强不息的精神，对后世知识分子产生了深远的影响。

Contemporary interpretation:

Born of a poor family, Confucius experienced much adversity and many ordeals. Yet he blamed none and reached the acme of wisdom through unwavering learning and searching. His spartan fortitude proves an indelible influence on subsequent scholars.

7. 子在齐，闻《韶》，三月不知肉味，曰："不图为乐之至于斯也！"

今 译

孔子在齐国听到《韶》的乐章,在三个月长的时间里,连吃肉都尝不出味道。他感叹地说:"想不到音乐的力量竟会有这么大。"

Translation:

The Master heard Shao music by Emperor Shun in the State of Qi and for three months he could not find delectation in delicious meat. He exclaimed, "The magic of music is beyond me!"

新 解

孔子喜爱音乐,在欣赏尽善尽美的《韶》乐时,完全沉浸在音乐的美妙境界,竟然吃饭都吃不出滋味。这段描写孔子对音乐的爱好简直到了入迷的地步,难怪孔子那么重视音乐对人的教育功能。确实,艺术能丰富人性,能够移人性情,不可不重视。

Contemporary interpretation:

Music was a passion of Confucius. When he was enjoying the consummate music of Shao, he was so intoxicated with the pleasure it produced that he had no appetite for food. The story reveals Confucius infatuation with music. And this explains his consistent emphasis of the educational function of music. Arts, indeed, could enrich and purify the innate humanity. Their importance must be fully recognized.

> 8. 叶公问孔子于子路，子路不对。子曰："女奚不曰，其为人也，发愤忘食，乐以忘忧，不知老之将至云尔。"

今 译

叶公向子路了解孔子的为人，子路不回答。孔子说："你为什么不这样说：'他这个人呀，发愤时忘记了吃饭，快乐时忘记了忧愁，不知道衰老将要到来，如此罢了。'"

Translation:

The Governor of Ye asks Zilu what kind of person the Master is. Zilu hesitates. Later the Master gets to know this and says to Zilu, "You could have said: 'This is my teacher: so studious as to forget hunger, so happy as to be carefree, so insouciant as to be oblivious of his senescence.'"

新 解

这段话相当于孔子的"自画像"，很风趣形象。他说自己在未得知识以前，好学不厌，几至废寝忘食的地步，可见其学习之刻苦。其次，在得到知识后，快乐得忘记忧愁，可见其乐道而不忧贫，为人旷达。第三，努力学习而不知老之将至，可见其自强不息的精神风貌。孔子这种"活到老,学到老"、毕生勤奋的学习态度令人感动。

Contemporary interpretation:

This statement could be seen as a witty self portrait of Confucius. Working hard and forgetting hunger reveals his industry; being happy and forsaking worries reveals his magnanimity; persevering in learning and ignoring his senescence reveals his enterprise. Confucius' "live and learn" attitude is really moving and worthy of emulation.